N

W

WATERCOLOURS

Table I

JAN VAN HUYSUM
Flower Piece
Aquarelle
Graphische Sammlung Albertina, Vienna

WATERCOLOURS

Edited and introduced by Per Amann with contributions by

Heribert Losert, Max Doerner and Hans Gert Müller

Artline Editions

Translated by Stephen Gorman

© 1989 by Berghaus Verlag — D-8347 Kirchdorf/Inn
English Language Rights: Artlines UK Ltd, 2 Castle Street
Thornbury, Bristol. Avon, England
Printed in West Germany — Imprimé en Allemagne
ISBN 1 871487 19 6

CONTENTS

Introduction

In Regard to the History of Aquarelles

The oldest paintings with water soluble colours, which we have documentary evidence of, are the Stone Age paintings in the caves of Lascaux and Altamira. These partly scratched rock paintings are coloured with natural materials: coloured clays, soot, etc. The early Chinese culture also knew how to use natural, water soluble, coloured minerals and clays. These were occasionally fired to achieve stronger hues. When we disregard the transparent natural colours which were used in ancient cultures, as for example in India, Egypt, and Greece, and that fresco paintings and book illuminations would be unthinkable without water colours, then we have the real beginning of our occidental aquarelle paintings with the existence of the most important German artist — with Albrecht Dürer. With his work, aquarelle becomes a definition in art.

He was the only artist in his time who found landscape and still life a worthy subject for water colour and who created fully valid aquarelles for several years; paintings from water soluble colours which were in beauty, in minute detail and in composition in no way inferior to the usual oil paintings. Colouring of sketches was usual for artists who lived before and after him, but the self-contained aquarelle is unparalleled in his work.

We do not know what made Albrecht Dürer choose water colours, known from ancient cultures, as a medium for independent works of art. There are many thoughts on art theories in Dürer's treatise but none on the aquarelle. Possibly an essay on landscape painting would have given us an elucidation. Unfortunately this work is lost. Art historians only know of its existence from a comment by Willibald Pirkheimer.

The series of water colours from Albrecht Dürer begins with the small painting of the infant Jesus, done in 1492 on parchment. It is painted in a masterly fashion and technique, in tempera with fine miniature brushes. Following this, there are several landscapes from the vicinity of his home around Nuremberg; for example, the "Drahtzieh" mill, a very interesting work, although in composition and colour still rather tentative. But the comprehension of the landscape, the special technique of the aquarelle was, for Dürer, already common knowledge in this work. As we have to assume that there was nothing which he could use for stimulation or as an example, this is an incredible testimony of his genius. One just has to think of the famous paintings from 1502 and 1503, "Turf", "Hare", or "Akeley", all created from water- and water soluble paints, insurpassable and unequalled in every aspect.

The age after Dürer was not good for aquarelles. Although the masters of the Danube School had a great disposition for landscapes, the fragrant frivolity of water colours was remote from their desires. Only Albrecht Altdorfer painted with water colours although they were body colours as used before in book illuminations. Altdorfer used these paints to colour in quill sketches.

The aquarelle was rediscovered in the Netherlands towards the end of the 16th century. Adriaen van Ostede, for example, produced very alluring genre paintings, mostly peasant scenes, and Hendrijk Averkamp was a master in the delightful presentation of groups of people in landscapes and of the life and work on the frozen canals in winter. The portrayal of everyday triviality, embellished with humour and fitted into the usual surroundings, was the strong-point of the Dutch painters. Art always has a close interrelation with the period and with the inner needs of people. So as an industrious, economically successful middle-class evolved in the Protestant North provinces of the Netherlands, a need was created for works of art which would appeal to their understanding and disposition. The withdrawal of the church as an employer and the lack of a representative sovereign made the middle-class circles the only potent customers. As one can see from the qualitative and quantitative development of Dutch painting, these buyers filled in the gap more than enough. Certainly there were suddenly no religious works or portraits of high-ranking people but true to life scenes, genre pictures, portraits of middle-class people, and, increasingly, landscapes. Naturally the aquarelle found its main area of use in smaller format with all kinds of presentation, though chiefly in genre pictures and later, increasingly in popular flower still lifes.

The Dutch painters can be regarded as the conveyors of aquarelle painting to England. The late transparent ink drawings of Anthony van Dyck, who created large paintings in the service of the Spanish throne in the Southern Catholic provinces of the Netherlands, were painted in London, where he spent his remaining years as a well respected court artist. His aquarelles of landscapes and of his fellow countrymen were an inspiration and example for artists such as Turner and Bonington. The mild air and melting atmosphere of the Dutch Lowlands found an enhancement on the other side of the English Channel and there became, in a much greater way, a bearing element of a newly created, very successful and exciting form of aquarelle. The English paintings of the 17th century would have been considerably more barren if it had not been for the tendency of the British weather to veil all contours in a kind of mist. This is especially

Table II

ALBRECHT DÜRER
The Saviour as a Child, 1492
Miniature on parchment
Graphische Sammlung Albertina, Vienna

true for the development of aquarelle painting and, to an even greater extent, for Turner who managed to bring across the characteristics of the soft flowing water colours into his oil paintings.

One can hardly imagine a greater contrast than the one between the distinguished Bonington and William Turner, both of whom belonged to the same generation. A typical example of the different approach are paintings of Venice by both artists. Bonington, fascinated by the impressive buildings of the lagoon city, painted an exact replica of the Ducal Palace with all the comings and goings on the jetty in front with its crowds of people, in short, from a historical viewpoint, a very interesting work full of the vitality of the era. Turner, on the other hand, had a completely different attitude towards the theme. Almost ten years before, in 1819, he had painted an aquarelle of Venice with a view of the Giudecca and San Giorgio in the rising sun. It is a very intimate piece of work, a web of light and atmosphere. The typical silhouette of the city serves as a small, bright, dividing line between a rippled water surface and an extremely lively sky. This picture is a symphony of colour, detached from the world, and decades ahead of its time. Richard Park Bonington was especially interested in landscapes with buildings. The aquarelle was his chosen technique. When he died in 1828, aged only 26, he left behind him a comprehensive collection of paintings, mainly works from France and from his travels in Italy. William Turner's aquarelles were also, to a great extent, works which he painted during his travels, although in his studio he also dedicated himself consequently to painting in water colour. He was involved lifelong in the portrayal of the elements, the drama and behaviour of nature, the fluctuation of light and air, movement and calmness. Painting true to life was not so essential to him, other aspects were more important, mainly Goethe's Theory of Colours which engaged his attention for a long time. Several of his earlier paintings were thought assimilations and symbolical representations of Goethe's perceptions. In this way, Turner went ahead of the conventional form in many of his aquarelles of Venice. He brought colour and light to the forefront and made them the major subject of the painting. In his studio, the sketches from his travels became inspired paintings without any topographical relationship. Although he was highly regarded because of the subject matter of his painting, Turner had to experience that the most important parts of his work were misunderstood from an artistic point of view; they were regarded as unfinished and unaccomplished. It was the new perception of the Impressionists, whose imminence he guessed but did not experience in spite of living to a high age, which created an understanding of his exceptional later work.

The 18th and 19th centuries were the great time of the traveller's aquarelle. All of society's high ranking travellers allowed artists to accompany them on their educational journeys and expeditions, where it was the artist's task to sketch or paint interesting scenes. This development started at the beginning of the 18th century especially in England, where not only paintings of the local landscapes were in demand but also pictures which the traveller had brought home from his Grand Tour. Italy was also for the English the favoured destination. The charm of the countryside was well known outside Italy's borders through Canaletto. "Alexander Cozens became an artistic pioneer. He had brought a sketch-book with him from Italy which served him as artistic inspiration for the rest of his life. This is important: although his pictures show far-reaching, fantastic visions, they are for the main part visions gained from the perceptible world; the borders are indistinct. In principle, Turner did not do anything different later. What he saw in reality became the motivation for the description of mood and drama, and within a half a century was imbued in fantastic colourfulness." (Koschatzky)

Thomas Gainsborough found a way to make landscape painting lighter and more lively in that he overcame the realistic style of the Dutch. But within a short time the aquarelle was regarded as an equal to the oil painting, mainly through the intensive encouragement from laymen who were interested in art. There were more than a dozen significant artists under the influence of Dr. Thomas Monro, a physician full of enthusiasm for art, who received his promotion. The main personalities from this circle were Thomas Girtin and William Turner. While Turner was, as mentioned, a pioneer and decisive stimulant for modernism, Girtin was important for his contemporaries. He made the decisive steps in the exploration of the artistic possibilities of the water colour. Another English artist gained importance for the development of the aquarelle: John Constable exhibited his work in 1824 in the Paris Salon and became the conveyor of a new stimulus for the young French artists around Delacroix.

From 1800 onwards, several organizations in England especially took up promotion of the aquarelle, after artists as well as collectors had realized that presentation and publicity in the usual academic exhibitions always disfavoured water colours which were mainly of a subdued constitution. The last exceptional artist who used this technique to a greater extent was James A. McNeill Whistler, an American who lived mostly in Paris, but whose work can be accounted to the English circle. Whistler died in 1903 by which time the English water colour painting had ceased to be important. France and the new spirit of Impressionism had taken over.

The German romantic period was an era in which the aquarelle with its specific intensity of expression had to be meaningful. Strangely though, the technique was only used by Philipp Otto Runge to any great extent for independent works of art. Caspar David Friedrich used water colours mainly for sketches, but also in many cases body colours. His conscientiousness in painting, his fine lining, and his love for detail led him with all his tendency to landscapes — the real domain of the aquarelle — to a preference for oil painting, although his graphical work is rich in aquarelles, drawings and mixed techniques. But here we are dealing with snapshots, kept, as it were, for later use in larger compositions.

Less important artists of the time were, on the other hand, excellent aquarellists, e. g. Joseph Anton Koch or Johann Adam Klein. In Vienna, the work of the highly gifted Rudolf von Alt stood out, whereas in Berlin Adolf Menzel upheld his great skill in this field until the end of the 19th century. His speciality was a masterly combination of opaque and aquarelle painting. Parallel to these artists from the German speaking countries, interesting developments began in France.

Eugène Delacroix, born in 1798, became the undisputed master of the French romantic period — and a favoured aquarellist. Admittedly, he wanted his aquarelles to be regarded above all as drafts, but quite often his sketches were put to paper with such enthusiasm, so immediately convincing in line and colour, that the oil paintings in which these first aquarelles later appeared as details tend to look insipid.

The romantic period in France was different from Germany where the yearning for the "Blaue Blume", a sociopolitical fraternity, was foremost. The aggressive adversaries of classicism, which had made the glorification of Napoleon and his thoughts on an empire a main theme, allowed the style of painting to become disparately more realistic and brought about a completely different choice of subject. The German romantics were looking for new values which would serve as a shield against the rising materialism of the philosophy of the natural sciences. Although C. D. Friedrich was likewise deeply moved by the ideas of the fighters for independence, his limited themes could not be compared to the directness of Delacroix.

Gustave Moreau was another artist who personified French art in the 19th century which, although highly interesting, had been neglected for a long time. Being put in one class with the symbolists, with no tendency towards Impressionism and coming from the academic tradition, he was regarded by the surrealists as one of their founders. His early larger pictures with classical themes brought him fame. In later years he tended towards a style of painting full of unprecedented nuance and delicateness of colour. He once said: "Colour has to be thought, imagined and presented." In his later paintings, he was involved with lascivious female figures, "symbolical deities of the indestructable lust". Pictures which he allowed to be exhibited were composed to the last detail, full of conceived symbolism and hidden meaning. Innumerable studies, sketches and drafts were adopted. These preparatory works are the ones which we should centre our attention on, as a large part of these sketches consist of delightful aquarelles. Odilon Redon, who brought the glowing colours, the themes and especially the interest in aquarelle painting into the 20th century, learned from their quality. Moreau's sketches also show that he was a significant pioneer of fauvism. Rouault, Matisse and Marquet are indebted to him for colour and subject matter.

The small village of Barbizon in the vicinity of Fontainebleau, surrounded by idyllic countryside, became a centre for artists towards the middle of the last century. A group of young artists — later called the "Barbizon School" — helped a whole generation towards a new relationship to and understanding of nature. Through Eugène Boudin, Camille Corot and Gustave Courbet, the artists from Barbizon became the direct instructors of the Impressionists; and Johan Barthold Jongkind, who worked with and learned from Boudin, became among these artists the most significant aquarellist. The Impressionists had their basis in the style of painting "en plein air", as represented by the Barbizon School. From there, they could find their way to colour.

Impressionism — the name was originally used in a very negative way by an opponent of this style of painting — became the first style common to a large group of artists on the threshold of modernism. At the same time, it is until now the only style of the modern movement whose basis can be grasped easily by the people of today without any great interpretation or background knowledge. Today it is difficult to understand that an art trend which represented a lively, colourful form of art was shown enmity. The breaking away from reproducing a form true to life in a picture, as practised by the Impressionists, is immaterial to us today. However, to the contemporaries of the Impressionists it appeared to be a mockery, an unreasonable demand to abolish light-heartedly what to that date had been regarded as the justification of art.

The impressionistic artists discovered the independent power of pure colour as an element of creation and gave it a major role in their pictures in its connection with light and air. The theme of the picture, which until then had been regarded as the real reason for the painting, became secondary. Impressionism renounced everything to do with contents, thoughts and sentimental, or moral expression, which till that time had been successful, and pronounced the subject matter unimportant. The outside coverings of things in a flickering light, the atmosphere — these were the things to be produced. The realization of impressions became the purpose of art.

The many changing influences which have an effect on the way an object appears became the essentials of their art. The impression of a moment, of every cloud, of every wind, altered by the changing sunlight, had to be kept. It was no wonder that aquarelle painting rose to considerable importance; the good range of colour as well as the possibility of working rashly made it the optimal technique. The comparatively small possibilities of working precisely and in detail were not regarded as a drawback by the Impressionists. Water colours became, especially in the early draft stages, a favourite medium. Of course, public opinion in France stood in the way of the technique; French exhibition organizers demanded oil paintings. An active, interested circle of art sponsors who especially favoured the small aquarelle never existed in France contrary to England.

This strange reticence from the art trade was also responsible for the fact that the aquarelle and gouache paintings from the great French artists were comparatively under-represented in their own country. The large art galleries are only dedicated to oil paintings while graphic collections are often denied the aquarelle as an expensive original for financial reasons. This is why especially private collectors in Switzerland and in the U.S.A. own exceptional masterpieces. Admittedly, there are several impressionistic artists in whose works aquarelles and gouache paintings play such an important part that official authorities have not been able to ignore them.

The first group of young artists who came together were Camille Pissaro, who orientated himself to Corot first of all, Paul Cézanne, Armand Guillaimin and Claude Monet. Monet brought Renoir, Sisley, and Bazille, who were his friends, into the group. Monet, who had painted together with Boudin and Jongkind, conveyed to the community that deep understanding of landscape and landscape section which is characteristic of the early aquarelles and oil paintings of the Impressionists. It is this direct transfer of the flair of the moment which makes the viewer want to be drawn into the picture and which he can still relive today.

Seurat and Signac carried the inherent thoughts of Impressionism further and finally came to an almost complete disintegration of the form in favour of colour. They composed their paintings with absolutely no contours, but built them up with a series of dabs of colour, placed next to each other. Other artists, especially Cézanne and Renoir, came to realize that, although the new colours were important, the form and also the balanced composition of the picture were of considerable relevance.

It was a disclosure, indeed a revelation, for several of the young French artists to discover works from the Japanese in the second half of the 19th century — especially coloured woodcuts which were arousing because of their colours and graphics. They brought a completely new understanding of space, line and coloured surface. The influence of this foreign art was very noticeable with van Gogh, Toulouse-Lautrec and Gaugin, but especially in the aquarelles of the young painters Bonnard and Vuillard. The transparency of the Japanese woodcut came very close to the aquarelle, and the individual characteristics of the lining and use of space was tempting for those who were always looking for new forms.

The improvisation of aquarelle painting especially interested the post-Impressionists. Firstly, the technique was eminently suitable for capturing the vitality of life. Secondly, the artists were interested in reducing the subject matter to its essential, which is also a domain of the aquarelle painting, as its suitability for detail is limited. The young artists endeavoured to capture the instants of everyday life and went further than just playing with light and air. They attempted to bring people into their art. Their predecessors had been rather indifferent to man and his problems. As landscape painters, they had no relationship to form. People were, at the most, decorative appendages to bring some movement into certain sections of the painting, equal to houses and haystacks. The thing which moved the Impressionists was the atmosphere and the play of light on a surface, whether it was bark or skin. The young generation, however, could not ignore the social crises and tensions of the age. An inner necessity made them take a stand, allowed the imponderable things of life to flow into their work. They were unable to draw back into their artistic problems and at the same time ignore human tragedy.

Emanating from Gaugin, a young group of artists who called themselves "Nabis" (i. e. Hebrew: the enlightened) endeavoured a contained form, impression, composition and intellectual content of painting, using the new colourfulness of Impressionism. Most of these demands came about in the knowledge that they were a contrast to the impressionistic view. The graphics and aquarelles of the Nabis are good examples of the social consciousness of the artists: Bonnard and Vuillard showed sympathy for the social conflict of their environment in their paintings of street scenes and groups of people. Although van Gogh was an artistic "loner", he was emotionally connected with thoughts of the group. His paintings were a crying witness of the inhuman situation of the working class, but the dramatic demands of the time are most obvious in the work of Toulouse-Lautrec. He dived into the milieu of prostitutes and souteneur and was eminently capable and willing to caricature, not with any evil intent, but excitable and deeply involved. Beside him, Steinlen and Bottini became "sympathetic, sometimes bitter witnesses of an especially difficult epoch in which several of them, and not the most insignificant, sheltered the wish to serve ideas and a moral rather than aesthetics." (R. Cogniat)

Gaugin and van Gogh, who started as Impressionists, continued the style of their art, enriched and altered it, and eventually developed beyond it to new forms and a new impulsive colourfulness. They became pioneers of expressionism and of the Fauves.

In Germany, Impressionism actually found relatively few artists who represented its interpretation and colour palette in their work: One of them was Lovis Corinth who was strongly influenced by Rubens. Impressionism was an important stage in his development, but with his later works he came to the same conclusions as the Fauves without actually belonging to the group. Max Liebermann was a very important representative of Impressionism in Germany. He still painted in Barbizon and learned a lot from Monet and expecially Degas. The colours in his later work resemble Degas'. Thirdly, we have Max Slevogt who came from the Munich academy and who was a passionate aquarellist. Of course many artists had contact with the French Impressionists, but this connection was more important for the development of the individual artist and less meaningful for the further development of Impressionism in regard to the history of art.

In Germany, as in France, another powerful movement originated after the turn of the century: expressionism. It meant more than an aesthetic tendency, it was a basic moral attitude, the logical consequence of a deliberate break with tradition. Expressionism is an artistic document of the breakdown of a hollow society. Its message to present an expression without compromise, to paint, carve, and sculpt similar to an unarticulated scream and disregarding any exterior form was a great necessity for many young people who had an interest in art. The founders and main representatives of this new style, the artist communities "Brücke" and "Der Blaue Reiter" drew many other artists into the spell of expressionism, e. g. Max Beckmann and Otto Dix.

"The aquarelle must appear to be an ideal medium for those young artists who want to free art from the bonds of history and the academies in order to revive it from their own experiences which force the artists to spontaneously paint in strong colours. The supple paintbrush with water colour could retain the transient impressions much more directly than other graphic techniques apart from drawing and lithography." (Leopold Reidemeister)

As a matter of fact, it was three students of architecture, Ernst Ludwig Kirchner, Erich Heckel and Karl Schmidt-Rottluff, who brought a completely new element into aquarelle painting with their style. Large areas of colour, hard in contrast, with contours quite black and overemphasized, and an overflowing urgency to show internally recognized connections externally. The three artists founded the artists' community "Brücke". Drawn by a blazing proclamation cut in wood and thus complying with the new style, Max Pechstein and Otto Mueller joined the circle as did Emil Nolde and Cuno Amiet for a short time.

A second circle of like-minded artists came together in Munich. A young group of painters congregated around the editors of an art almanac, which had been founded and published by Wassilij Kandinsky and Franz Marc and had the name of a (lost) painting by Kadinsky, "Der Blaue Reiter". These artists were looking for a new form and real content in art. August Macke, Alexej von Jawlensky, Paul Klee, and Heinrich Campendonk, also Gabriele Münter and Marianne von Werefkin were the core of the group. From time to time, they were joined by outsiders with similar views. Aquarelle painting played a major role in their work. August Macke's most enchanting compositions were achieved with this technique whereas Kandinsky and Klee went further; they accomplished the changeover to abstract painting with their many aquarelles. It was also Der Blaue Reiter who made contact with a group of French artists who worked together under the nom de guerre "Les Fauves".

A Paris critic had tried to disqualify the young artists as wild animals — fauves. Henri Matisse and his combatants Derain, Marquet, Vlaminck, Rouault and Dufy and for a short time also von Dongen and Braque attempted with pure colours to build up a brilliant firework display of placard type paintings, in opposition to all naturalism and without spaciousness or plasticity. Only Matisse remained true to the standard of form, which soon developed, and never left the exciting colours which he inserted full of clarity, serenity and balance. Rouault became engrossed in earth's heaviness, Dufy became a serene storyteller. All artists from the beginning of modernism found their way to individual development.

The change in the individual creative periods in the life and works of Pablo Picasso can be especially seen. From his cubist time to the time of his classical detached paintings, complete changes were effected, not only stylistically but also in his technique and picture composition. This development is not obvious in the use of a specific technique as the painting materials were used differently and with varying preference. The aquarelle played a rather small role with Picasso, he seldom used the technique and mostly prefered gouache.

Summing up and looking back it can be said that painting with water colours, whether pure aquarelle, gouache or tempera, has undergone the same changes in style as, for example, oil painting or graphic art. There are, however, the extensive possibilities of variation of the aquarelle with many different mixed techniques. Generous aquarelles can be found where fragrant areas of colour are placed on top of a sketch draft or pure colour compositions in which accent has been added later with the quill or pencil. There are accurately composed pictures, which have just been painted with a pointed brush and transparent colour, and others where the wet colours have run together. In this technique colours can be used which are layed on top of each other, raised to an overpowering luminosity, sprayed colour, brushed colour and many, many more possibilities. Christian Rohlfs, for example, was an excellent master of ingenious mixed techniques. He devoted a great part of his work to the aquarelle painting and constantly discovered new effects.

Aquarelle painting is an exceptionally interesting technique for the artist as well. There is no other form of art where the creative process is so obvious and accessible, as the pure aquarelle hardly allows any correction. Once a colour has been placed, it cannot be changed but only toned. This assumes a certain intimacy of the artist with his colour and at the same time lets the grace of a "light hand" be seen.

Ultimately, it is the attraction of the natural flow of colour and the extensive lack of exactly reproduced detail which excites the viewer, who unconsciously completes what is missing. The choice of colour puts across the mood, while brushstrokes and accent give the picture theme, where the sketchy impression, which would be regarded in an academic sense as unfinished, is quite often the substance of the painting. But even aquarelles which are completed to perfection and which can in their elaboration be compared to oil paintings convey the pleasing agility which is characteristic of this technique.

Table III

ALBRECHT DÜRER
Akeley
Water colours and opaque colours on parchment
Graphische Sammlung Albertina, Vienna

"There has always been an interaction between art and pedagogics," the artist Heribert Losert once wrote, "each cultural epoch seems to have been affected to a great extent by the respective form of this relationship. But never have the questions about art education or, in fact, the educational values in art been so pressing as in the present situation, in which humanity constantly seems to be threatened. So the fine arts will also become, especially today, a healing factor, since the nature of the arts has a surprising similarity to the manifold substance of life; a consideration of the precepts of life is always a necessary postulate for a sensible education." To create artistic freedom for adults, to lead them to an extension of their own being by virtue of artistic ability and pedagogical insight is a concern of Heribert Losert, which he has transmitted in his painting courses for decades.

In the following pages, the artist gives an insight into the way such a course runs. The editor finds this educational excursion a definite enrichment of the theme in the supposition that this book especially appeals to people who are interested in aquarelles and who dabble in art themselves. It is very fortunate that this contribution comes directly from the view of the artist himself.

In Praise of Water Colour
Experiences in a Painting Course by Heribert Losert

Today, creativity allows us to discover many varieties, one has the choice of old and new materials. Water colours are one of the most used and develop more and more into a form of expression which meets the demands of modern concerns. Already the handling of the material shows its aptitude for artists and laymen. The many possibilities of use suit its inherent nature: an incredible transparency is revealed here, no matter how intensely it is used.

Painting with water colours stimulates the spontaneity and at the same time accuracy, which also seems valuable to us in the educational field. In state schools, however, we are looking for appropriate departments in vain most of the time: there are not enough tutors who are able to convey the technical and manual skills. Common opinion, that water colours are only useful for sketching and that they cannot be corrected, is certainly based on a misunderstanding. Certainly, they demand a more distinguished technique from the robust body colours, modifications which should be followed the same as the rules of a game. The consequences should be acknowledged, especially when using transparent layers of colours. This technique has to be carried out more continuously than painting wet in wet. When colours are used on top of each other, the state of the colour underneath must be considered, whereby the wet-in-wet technique obviously suits a more uninterrupted form of creation. White paper is the ideal ground, it allows the finest colour changes in painting, and, as every tone remains present, it makes a rich differentiation of the whole possible. Such a combination, with regard to the individual item, becomes the characteristic feature of a creative process, a concern which is worthy of notice not just in painting courses.

Upheavals in society create new responsibilities for artists as well: in connection with educational and therapeutic problems, it shows above everything its social function. The powers of fantasy and abilities, which threaten to perish in today's professional life, can only receive the necessary care through appropriate initiatives. Courses in which painting with water colour can be practised should certainly not be missing. This description of a course in aquarelle painting, even though incomplete — even the most detailed correspondence course cannot replace personal tuition —, should be informative and serve as stimulation, since the question of using one's spare time sensibly is more vital today than ever before. Apart from evening courses in adult education and from the Waldorf schools, there are also private vacation colleges which have to be mentioned in this context as well.

A harmony of relaxation and creativity is the basic concept of an educational institution in which one expects, in a sense, healing apart from practical instruction. The participants of the painting courses which take place in summer come from different walks of life and age groups. The artistically gifted should be able to practise next to the beginner, since such contrasts sometimes act as a motive power in development. Being together and aiming for the same thing allows the student to forget about everyday life; he has a fixed programme which starts with introductory exercises. The actual play begins with the setting up of the background. This is a simple process, but one which gives all involved a feeling of curious expectancy. The moist, wavy paper has to be stretched as tight as a drumskin. Even watering down the paint is not regarded completely factually nor is the process of layering, but rather more as a puzzle, as fitting pieces of a still unknown motif.

The series of obligatory themes begins with the representation of blue and yellow, a combination of two colours which demonstrates not only their specific expression but also the corresponding painting technique. That is why all distracting references to content are avoided in such an exercise; the student should learn to "listen" to the colour. The question of 'how' should become more important than the question of 'what'. Above all, blue should be mentioned in the educational field; it is more suitable than any other colour for creating picture structures full of tension. With its incomparable transparency it allows incredible varieties. At the same time it remains passive, recedes with its darkness, and becomes surroundings and background to the lighter areas which can then stand out so much more clearly. With this first exercise, we discover a phenomenon of a colour perspective which surprises us again and again. Transparent colours, which start at the margin of the painting as a dark shade and which become lighter towards the centre, have a sparkling lustre which reminds us of crystals. The blank white areas of paper lose their materialistic appearance and become more and more the expression of a quality of light. In the opposite concentration of colour, dark towards the centre — one just has to think of thunder clouds and inkspots —, the blue would be disturbing and upsetting.

To show yellow, one needs different structures: This colour is equivalent to a bright light, which appears in central concentrations: as in floating individual forms with disintegrating edges. The surrounding white also plays an important role. Water here becomes a supporting element, mainly in the wet-in-wet technique which we now try out for the first time, as an interlude so to speak. The participants see this as a welcome chance after their exercise in blue. In anticipation of later use, they presently concern themselves with the creation of a background with mainly fluctuating arrangements which can most successfully and quickly be achieved by moving the painting back and forwards. Such movements allow a controlled running together of the colour, the ''steering'' of a chance occurence which should not be ruled out in aquarelle painting. Although this experiment is fascinating, we decide that working with contrasting colours is more important. This is the reason why we return to the layer technique again.

A third colour, green, is created when yellow and blue overlap. It enlivens the painting, but blue and yellow alone cannot produce a satisfying timbre. The incorporation of red allows the achievement of a full harmony. This colour should only appear in a few places at first, as it is rather intense and causes an optical change of its surroundings with minimal usage. For example, a cold blue would be severely affected by the proximity of red areas; only the broken colours, which are warmed by red, such as violet, brown, or olive green can build a bridge to blue. The use of transparent colours again brings the opposite into a reasonable realationship. Such a transparent colour structure will allow — similar to polyphonic phrases — the individual colour choice to be recognized in the harmony. One shade of colour alone can have decisive consequences: if, for example, from a complementary contrast of two colours a quality contrast is formed by the addition of a third. Gradual mixing increases the remaining tones more and more; in each of these results, source and process are revealed.

New tasks can be developed from all the previous ones. In the end, the harmony will lead to concrete themes which should find their obvious expression in the congruence of colour and form. The exercises become more free and varied: but, as before, simply formed areas function as a medium for the colour; the vertical and the horizontal form the framework. Especially worthwhile is the expression of coloured poles such as ''warm and cold'' or ''positive and negative'', also themes such as ''interior'' and ''Southern town'', but still conceived in a tectonic and abstract concept. The motifs become more and more related to reality with the following wet-in-wet painting which we practise at full length. Hence subjects are determined to a great extent by the surrounding landscape: plain, stream, hills, and clouds are favourite motifs.

The sense of colour which was developed with layering is also useful in the second aquarelle technique. The colours do not mix anymore on their own as with the transparent layers; the required shade of colour has to be mixed on the palette, the running together of the colour on moist sheets of paper requires quick reactions. Both techniques supplement each other in a harmonious way. While transparent painting involves more patience and care, the spontaneity is quite often the decisive factor in wet-in-wet painting. Of course painting "out of the colour" has to be learned first, but even the smallest step can contribute as a road marking in the achievement of this aim.

Occasional discussions about problems with form and expression of modern art are also a part of the complete programme. Who would not enjoy in such a contemplation the aquarelles from a journey to Tunisia and Klee's words: "That is the significance of a happy hour; I and the colour are as one ..." Such enthusiasm is not only given to the great; the pupil knows to appreciate the favour of such moments as well. Sometimes the pleasure in the beautiful is enough to free energies which could enrich our lives persistently. Hence the real success of such a painting course does not lie as much in providing knowledge and manual abilities, but in encouraging a kind of self-discovery. A perception of the transparency here experiences its deeper meaning.

Admirers of aquarelle painting are always interested in the technical rudiments of this art form. This occasioned the editor to add a text to this book which contains everything worth knowing for the manual accomplishment of this interesting and attractive art genre. The following contribution from Hans Gert Müller is an excerpt from "Malmaterial und seine Verwandlung im Bilde" (15th edition 1980, published by Ferdinand Enke — Stuttgart) from the Nestor of research into colour, Professor MAX DOERNER. This article informs extensively about painting with water colours and about the technique of aquarelle and gouache.

Aquarelle Painting

The paint particles in aquarelle colours only have a function in paint ready for use, in stored paints, and also during the process of painting. The particles only have to retain the working ability during storage and prevent a coagulation or flaking of the pigments. A criterium for good aquarelle colours is that the bonding agent does not enclose the pigments in a film nor stick them to the background paper. They have done their duty, when the coat of paint is dry. They diffuse into the background, into the paper, more completely, the more absorbent, i. e. the less sized, the paper is. The paper sucks up the very small pigment particles, it absorbs them. The paper fibre has been dyed, as this process was referred to by Hans Wagner. Thus the dainty appearance of a good aquarelle is created.

It is surprising that water colours do not contain a bonding agent in the sense of our earlier definition, although the painting medium contains non-volatile constituents. Chemists have an elegant expression for the non-volatile parts which prevent a flaking of the pigment particles. They call them "protective colloids" and do not go into the question of a bonding agent at all.

The peculiarities of aquarelle colours make it impossible to manufacture the paints oneself. Factories which make artists' paints use synthetic materials apart from natural emulsions such as ox gall; they also use gum arabic, tragacanth, and, less often, dextrin as a protective colloid. The solubility, especially of caked aquarelle colours, is ensured by the addition of small quantities of alcohols such as glycerine or glycol, or sometimes by the addition of syrup or sugar. In order to obtain the fine particle size of the pigments necessary for gentle transparent application, the manufacturers of artists' paints used to have to grind pigments in triple rollers. This was sometimes only successful at the expense of the beauty of the colour. Today finely dispersed, highly stable pigments which are almost in the colloidal range with their particle size are available. They are therefore especially suited for the pigmentation of aquarelle paints.

In aquarelle painting, the mixing of colours is especially easy with a transparent application of highly thinned down paint. There are skilled aquarellists who choose to work with a palette of not more than 7 to 9 colours.

Grounds and Painting Equipment

Aquarelle painting uses the transparent effect of colours which are applied very thinly.

Every transparent effect requires a light ground. In a pure aquarelle, all the light comes from the ground, which is in most cases paper. Parchment, ivory, silk, batiste, and also chalk or plaster grounds are used as well.

This ground has to be as white and free of oil and at the same time as constant as possible.

Papers. Hand-made paper from linen rags fulfills this demand, but not paper from cotton or wood. Hand-made paper can be identified by its uneven, uncut edges. Apart from this, it has certain watermarks which can be seen, when the paper is held to the light, and which verify the authenticity. Linen paper absorbs water well, allows fading, and the colour looks fresh on it.

For several years, paper-mills have been using cellulose for drawing paper, which is practically free of wood due to the way it is treated. Today, aquarelle paper is produced with a large percentage of rags and refined cellulose, which compares favourably with the quality of old rag-paper.

The colours appear optically more satisfactory and stick better on rough grained paper. The colour appears more lively and less compact, because the tone catches light and shadow in the small elevations and hollows.

The paper has to be sized entirely. Applied.colour must not run out when a corner of the paper is scraped. Aquarelle paper has to be free of alum, otherwise the paint coagulates easily. It should not contain fat, because then it does not take on the colour. Fat can be removed by rubbing the paper with thinned ox gall or with a thinned down ammonia solution.

Aquarelle paper should only leave 1—1,5% ash when burnt, otherwise it is weighted with clay or other filling materials.

The light fastness of the paper must be examined. A change in tone or yellowing of the paper puts the whole effect in question because of the thin application of colour. Sheets of paper should be left in a book, half exposed to the sun. After 14 days, the paper halves should not be different in colour if the paper is usable.

The paper should not be rolled. The result could be light cracks. Zinc white cracks and transparent varnishes do not lie evenly. Paper should therefore ideally be kept in a portfolio.

Aquarelle paper can normally be used from both sides. A distinction has to be made between normal painting and drawing paper for use in schools and for technical drawings and the first-class quality rag paper for artistic paintings.

Parchment paper is also used now and again as a ground for aquarelle painting. Real parchment does not fall apart when chewed. If necessary, it has to be freed from fat like aquarelle paper. Parchment paper is a dense cotton paper which has been treated with sulphuric acid and which is, of course, of inferior quality. Egg yolk and gum arabic on parchment are a basis for gilding.

The aquarelle paper is stretched on a board with tacks or pasted to a frame. In the latter case, the paper which is to be painted is moistened on the reverse side; the edges, which have been folded over, are then pasted and pressed flat. The paper becomes wavy when it is wet, is expands and then draws together again when dry. Attention has to be paid that no bits of paste are present either on the back or front of the surface which is to be painted.

Aquarelle blocks, available in various sizes, are practical as the tiresome stretching can then be saved, this also applies to devices for fixing the sheets in certain sizes.

The quality of the brush is very important in aquarelle painting. Red marten brushes are the best, apart from those, hake brushes and wide brushes for fading are also used.

The aquarelle brush must have a good point, must not split, it should have a wedge shape rather than a rounded appearance.

The brush should immediately be put into proper shape after washing so that the point does not suffer. The point has to be uncovered while drying. If individual hairs split, they should not be cut off. Instead, the brush is dipped in water and the protruding hairs are carefully burnt off. For very fine work, plover feathers can also be used.

Tin palettes painted white are the most appropriate, as they correspond to the ground.

Painting

Light pencil lines have to be sketched carefully, being careful not to erase or touch the area to be painted so that the paper is not damaged and the colour is absorbed evenly. The trained hand draws freely with the paint brush. The paper is moistened with a sponge and water is allowed to soak in slightly so that the surface does not appear wet and painting is begun immediately. Calcium-free water, if necessary boiled or destilled water, is the only painting medium. The choice of colours should be kept to a minimum, in this way the finished picture will appear all the more colourful. Most tones can be achieved with Indian yellow, madder red, Parisian blue, and sparkling chrome oxide green, and it is very seldom that other colours are needed as a supplement. When the student of water colour painting is sure of his or her abilities, colour can then be used in its full range and intensity, beginning preferably with shadow and gradually developing, tone in tone, to lighter areas. Freshness is all-important here, tortured colours are dirty and blunt.

In the older manner of aquarelle painting, application began with very thin, light, unexpressed, neutral shades and was gradually strengthened. Effects were achieved with a driving and running together of colour which does not appeal to modern taste anymore. Highlights had to be left blank, this gave the work a certain exciting attraction, a pleasurable, decorative, and harmonic effect. Fading, which is only possible on linen paper, or lifting the wet layer of colour with a brush, chamois, eraser, and the like, also allow highlights to be drawn out. These are, however, softer and more hazy than those left blank. Colours which have been put on dry paper form edges. These again may also be employed for useful effects, when they are taken into account from the beginning. This effect is used frequently in modern poster art.

Today, aquarelles are treated more freely. Following the method of Dutch artists, white is often used, it is added on semi-moist or dry paper. This produces either an airy, soft, or substantial effect. Aquarelles have a very transparent effect. The attraction of the aquarelle lies in the light, bright hues. To obtain a profounder impression of grey depths, some painters resort to an aquarelle varnish of 1 part Zapon varnish with 2 parts alcohol. Thinned, unglossy shellac fixative may also be used for this purpose.

Varnish should first be tried on a layer of ultramarine to see the effect. However, it is better to do without any of these varnishes altogether.

Combined with tempera, on good paper which has been pasted on a suitable background, water colours allow effects comparable to the Gothic painting in style, gradually changing from light to dark. Generally the white of the back-

Table IV

WILLIAM TURNER
Prudhoe Castle
Aquarelle, around 1826
British Museum, London

ground is kept and only increased slightly with tempera. Varnishing is done with thinned down mastic. Synthetic resins or varnishes may also be used here in an oil-free technique, as long as they do not yellow.

Ivory is also used as a base for water colour now and then, especially for miniatures. Ivory yellows when stored. This tinge can be removed if one places the ivory leaves between layers of blotting paper which have been soaked in hydrogen peroxide. Ivory is very sensitive to fat; the area to be painted should never be touched directly. Fat can be removed with petrol, thinned ammonia solution or ox gall. The area to be painted is scraped smooth and then polished with cork and very fine pumice powder and water or with an eraser. After washing it in water, it is left to dry between sheets of pure white blotting-paper. Fat-free tracing paper and a clean white underground have to be used for tracing. Painting is begun with light tones, stippled, wet into wet, but not too liquid so that edges do not form, and the colours appear as if from a mist. Painting should be started at the top of the paper, working to the bottom. There are old miniatures on ivory where strong local colour has been applied on the reverse side in thin oil colours which shine through. They are glazed only slightly and raised from the front. In some, a sheet of silver foil has been put behind, which gives all the colours a fullness and fine greyness.

Highlights can be left blank or colours can be brought out. The colour effect has to remain light and loose. Colours which are not genuine, such as tar colours, e. g. alizarin, or zinc yellow and Indian yellow, should not be used, because they are absorbed by the ground. A tone which has become too heavy can be brightened by scraping or lifting it off with a needle (under a magnifying glass). One should start with the simplest transparent tones. The brush has to be moist but not too wet nor full of paint. Red should be used very sparingly in skin tones, it is better to use it last. Grounding with an alum solution 1:10 or with a trace of glycerine allows a broader area of work.

Gouache

The aquarelle is considerably surpassed in the reality of the tones by gouache. Grey, airy hues emerge here, an effect similar to pastel, reached, however, with liquid paints. The gouache paintings from Adolf Menzel are the best example of this. Opaque colouring offers a much greater freedom and ease of treatment than the pure aquarelle.

The bonding agents here are the same as in aquarelle colours.

All the colours have white fillers, barite, clay, etc. or body colours added to them, as was mentioned with aquarelles.

Toned grounds, coloured paper, shaded canvas, etc. are more suitable for opaque painting than the white ground used for a transparent effect. Round bristle brushes and also hair brushes are the best. It is advisable to begin with a thin coating and then gradually increase the intensity, covering more intensely, preferably wet into wet, with or without the use of the ground shade, which gives eminently useful, harmonic tones when just slightly covered.

Highlights are put on thickly and half dry with very little bonding agent. This gives a very good, solid effect. An overall light atmosphere is created best with this technique.

Gouache can be fixed and made water resistant by dusting the painting with 4% gelatine and then fixing it with 2% formalin.

Today gouache is mostly replaced by tempera which is much more versatile. Poster paints are also widely used, basically a distemper with filler which covers well. Absolute water resistance is not demanded. It could only be obtained with distemper by fixing with 2% formalin, not, however, with rubber based paints.

Framing Aquarelles

When framing an aquarelle, attention should be paid to the gap between painting and glass; the paint should not touch the glass directly, nor should the paper rest on wood, otherwise it becomes stained. Eibner pointed out that zinc white has a destructive effect on certain colours if it is directly under glass. This is especially true for tar colours and in the presence of moisture. Therefore a gap of a few millimetres has to remain. Aquarelles should ideally be stored in portfolios. In any case, they should be protected from direct sunlight and dust.

ILLUSTRATIONS

Max Liebermann
1847 Berlin — 1935 Berlin

"Berlin, that means energy, intelligence, tightness, lack of sentimentality and romance, the absence of reverence for the past, modernism as a thing of the future, cosmopolitanism as an absence of Germanic emotion..." Thomas Mann wrote these words as a contribution to the 80th birthday of the painter Max Liebermann. Liebermann was a citizen of Berlin, an active interested artist, stimulated by the city for the whole of his life, a leading artist in the Berlin of the twenties.

Max Liebermann came from a respected factory-owning family belonging to the long-established Jewish community in Berlin. The family had already earned well from the cultural life in the city in the 19th century. His upper class origins gave Liebermann financial security as an artist all his life and gave him the aura of a man of the world. His solid personal and artistic training, his alert sympathy of heart, perseverance in his artistic aims, and last but not least his Prussian accuracy could also have made him a good diplomat or minister. He was a very imposing figure in the lively art circles. His incredible ability and geniality made him the most respected artist in Germany. He was, in his art, an uncompromising and indefatigable hard worker, but all this did not stop him being a helping friend at all times to other artists.

The decisive discovery in his artistic career was the work of the French Impressionists. In the paintings of Manet, Monet, and Cézanne, he found the ideas which brought him away from his habits of seeing things like the old masters, altered and freed his palette. Impressionism became for him a Weltanschauung, although his version bore the imprint of sober reflection, balance, and mental reserve. Objectivity towards nature and a truthfulness of form were the unshakable basis of his art. From here, he could open up to the colour and place his delicate brushstrokes.

Liebermann did not paint many aquarelles although he respected the technique especially for the opportunity it gave him to paint in an easy and rapid manner. In 1893 he wrote, "I believe it is a technique which is especially suitable for my way of representing nature." He did not often work outside, and here he preferred pastel. The chosen subjects for his aquarelles were interiors, people, or sometimes houses or streets.

Max Peiffer-Watenphul
1896 Weferlingen near Helmstedt — 1976 Rome

The artist first studied medicine and law and even graduated in church law, an area far removed from pictorial art. The turning point was a meeting with Paul Klee, who encouraged his artistic attempts and was responsible for his admission to the Bauhaus. Lyonel Feininger and Wassilij Kandinsky were his tutors, with their help he developed his artistic personality. Otto Dix, who he met in 1920 in Düsseldorf, had an influence on his work as well. But his travels, especially in Italy — which later became his home —, with all the impressions gained were mainly responsible for the characteristic features of his work. His ability to absorb experience made it unnecessary for Peiffer-Watenphul to paint while he was travelling, in fact that would have been hindering to him. Getting to know countries and people and taking them into his alert visual memory was enough. He visited Mexico and North Africa, Greece and, again and again, Italy. Impressions which he gained while travelling were kept in his consciousness and were some time later put to paper either deliberately or incidentally.

Peiffer-Watenphul received the Villa Massimo Prize in 1931 and 1932 finally settled in Italy. But in 1938, he received an appointment to the textile college in Krefeld and in 1942 to the college of arts-and-crafts in Salzburg. He complied with both callings. He settled again in Italy immediately after the war, first in Venice, then in 1956 in Rome which became his final home. In 1964 he was offered the chairmanship of the Salzburg summer academy as a successor to Oskar Kokoschka. He gladly accepted this honourable post, and many young artists were able to participate in his wealth of experience.

People or rather human forms play no part in the works of Max Peiffer-Watenphul. At the most, they appear in his larger paintings as small forms, as an accessory or as a lively point. His pictures are wide flowing landscapes, time and time again pine trees, Arcadian fields full of calmness, harmony, and Levantine grace. The paintings are ageless, static compositions of well balanced fortuity. The colours are subdued; actually the economical use of paint, broken and full of nuance, gives more a tone than a colour. His chosen themes are Southern house walls, Venetian palaces, landscapes with ruins, and views of decaying architecture. Aquarelle painting played a major role in his work, the light flowing colours were eminently suitable for his technique of painting.

Isaac Israëls
1865 Amsterdam — 1934 Paris

Isaac Israëls was the son of the most famous Dutch artist of the 19th century: Jozef Israëls. At the same time, he was the only painter from his country who can be completely ascribed to French Impressionism, if one ignores the fact that Vincent van Gogh, while still coming in contact with the Impressionists, cannot be regarded as belonging to the group. Israëls had an exceptional position in Dutch art. First of all, he painted in Charleroi, in the milieu of labourers from the glass-blowing factories, among people who lived in wretched conditions and who had to work extremely hard. Especially the Dutch church had drawn attention to the unbearable living conditions in the Borinage, the industrial area of Belgium. Vincent van Gogh had painted his socially accusing pictures in this industrial area five years before Israëls. They were shocking scenes in dark depressing colours. After all, van Gogh had acquired his knowledge of art and his gloomy melancholic colours from Isaac Israëls' father.

One year after his stay in Charleroi, the young Israëls went to Amsterdam where he lived in the house of G. H. Breitner, a Dutch Impressionist who influenced his choice of motif and theme (among other things, they had the same models). He also adopted a lot of his colouring. He painted street parties, scenes from revues and vaudeville, dance halls, and sailors' whores. During the summer, he met Max Liebermann who came to Scheveningen every year, since he was a friend of Israëls' father. The range of themes changed under his influence: he painted the beach, children playing, relaxed people at the sea. The gloomy-sensual demi-monde paintings stopped, and at the same time the colours changed, resembling those of his paternal friend.

In 1900, Israëls moved to Paris where he got to know the Impressionists and their novel colours and where he discovered his future models: the mannequins from the fashion studios. From now on, he changed his use of colours, renounced the style of light and shadow which he had learnt, and placed colour next to colour. He becomes the painter of the grisettes and milliners. He finds his girls, dressed in buoyant clothes, in fashion studios and night cafés, or the sauntering couples in the Bois de Boulogne. He becomes a shrewd observer of the world of elegance. With his delicate colours and his cultivated taste, he becomes a sharp observer of the elegant world, but without lapsing into fashion painting. With his psychologically sympathetic point of view, he almost matches the ingenuity of Toulouse-Lautrec.

The paintings on the following pages:

33
MAX LIEBERMANN
Venetian Alley, 1878
Aquarelle on cardboard. 24.7 x 15.6 cm
Hamburger Kunsthalle, Kupferstichkabinett

34/35
MAX PEIFFER-WATENPHUL
Porto d'Ischia, 1955
Aquarelle with pencil
Private collection

36
ISAAC ISRAËLS
Lady with a Cigarette, Reading
Aquarelle with charcoal sketching, 50.8 x 35.3 cm
Rijksmuseum Kröller-Müller, Otterlo

M. Liebermann   Venezia 9/10 78.

Emil Nolde
1867 Nolde — 1956 Seebüll

"Then I reached for water colours and painted the glowing red ball of the sun sinking over slush, I painted the white falling snow, and the finished and half-finished paintings were lying about, snowed over, so that I had to look for them. I was amazed at how the colours had set in a strange dreamy way under the snow. Sometimes I also painted in freezing evening hours and enjoyed seeing the frozen paints dry in crystal stars and rays on the paper. I loved such co-operation of nature; in fact, the whole solidarity with nature: the artist, reality, and painting."
(Emil Nolde, Jahre der Kämpfe)

Emil Nolde made the aquarelle a substantial part of his work as no other modern artist did. This technique accompanied him during all his life. He always found artistic problems which he wanted to solve with this medium — had to solve with this medium. It was those intensely coloured landscapes and flower aquarelles which gave the artist a place of honour with the general public as one of the most important German artists. Nolde's aquarelles are open to the viewer without any circumlocutary explanation. One can look at them and immediately be entranced by the luminous colours and the clear composition. At the same time, one is involved in the creative process, since the thoughts which moved the artist in the moment of action are obvious in an aquarelle painting. The transparency of the colours allow an understanding of the artistic intentions.

Emil Hansen, which is his original name, came from a Frisian peasant family. Although he was attracted to colour from an early age, the idea of his becoming an artist was completely foreign and unthinkable for his parents. He was, however, allowed to begin an apprenticeship in the carving school of a furniture factory. His years as a journeyman in his trade brought him to South Germany, and eventually the talented and industrious young man managed the leap to the St Gallen college of arts-and-crafts. Here he was given the lectureship for "ornamental drawing". Caricature postcards and Swiss mountains with troll faces, which he designed, sold surprisingly well to the tourists and earned him a reasonable sum of money, a fortunate circumstance which allowed him a certain amount of financial freedom. He was able to leave his post and make his first study trip. In Paris, he became a student in the Studio Julian as so many young German artists did in those years. He had a close look at the paintings of the great French artists and learned a lot from them. Still his stay in Paris was a time without any serious experiences. Since his nature was only open to Nordic culture, he kept a distance to this art. "He was a loner who remained completely on his own on his artistic path. His battle with outside and personal problems was fought without the clarifying dialogue with other like-minded people. He did without the support of the community of congenial artists in the struggle for the new art concept — expressionism." (C. Mosel)

The liberation to his own style of painting came about at the same time as his move to Berlin and marriage to Ada Vistrup, a Danish woman. Both these events were occasion for his taking the surname Nolde, an external sign for the birth of the artist so to speak. He bought a fisherman's cottage on the island of Alsen and built a small wooden beach studio. In spite of his financial need, the better working conditions and close contact with his beloved countryside enabled him to produce a series of grand paintings. A trip to Italy was made possible by friends. It was meant as a convalescence for his wife who suffered from ill health and as an encouragement to new creations. It brought, however, no noticeable stimulus for new activities. But immediately afterwards began the materially and artistically successful period in the life of the artist. Gustav Schieffer, who later became the chronicler of Nolde's graphics, entered his life. The Macaenas Karl Ernst Osthaus made the connection with the art patrons of the Rhineland, and a visit to him enabled a study of new French art in the collection in his house in Hagen. The members of the artists' association Brücke saw several of Nolde's paintings which were exhibited in Dresden. Karl Schmidt-Rottluff wrote to Nolde, asking him to join the group, as he recognized a similar direction in their efforts. Nolde gladly accepted. "The letter lay in a folio among the earliest graphic prints and drawings from the Brücke artists, it was at the time a surprise and an unusually great pleasure. I was not alone! There were also other artists looking forward to the future with pleasure, with aspirations similar to mine."

First of all, Schmidt-Rottluff worked together with Nolde by the sea, then Nolde went to Dresden. He made friends with the Brücke artists and joined the group, but only to leave again after a year. "It was difficult for me to bear the frictions in the human and artistic field which are possibly inevitable. I did not want the developing similarity of the artists, whose works quite often resembled each other. Again I went my artistic way alone. Our sentiments, however, stayed the same and I remained their friend in an artistic sense."

Following this, he worked intensively with woodcuts, work which had been inspired by the Brücke artists. Nolde wrote that he had experienced the printing of Brücke woodcuts as a stimulation: "through which I saw the self-printing of wooden plates, and soon cut a portfolio of figures from fairy tales. I had had enough experience in my five-year occupation in carving to handle the wood and to determine its character. I always allowed the different interesting grains and sometimes the knots to have a say in printing, several qualities which do not exist in linocuts, an artificial material which I never liked to use because of its lack of life."

Nolde was now enabled from different sides to hold exhibitions, including a large one in the art museum in Essen. Friends made it possible for him to take part in an expedition to New Guinea in the correct assumption that getting to know primitive cultures would bring him further. When he came back, right into the outbreak of war, he was able to purchase a small farmhouse near Ruttebüll to where he withdrew to during the war years. Eventually he was able to obtain the Seebüll farmstead in the middle of the 1920's. In 1927 he began to build his house and studio there. His great creative period began, always moving from his flat in Berlin in winter to the sea in summer. Nolde was admired and respected, a large circle of friends admired his work greatly. Optimal working and attractive living conditions gave him creative tranquility.

But this time of internal and external peace was not to last long. The disastrous political development was drawing close. In 1933, aged almost seventy, he became seriously ill. During his convalescence from a stomach operation he was increasingly exposed to political pressures which ended in 1937 with the seizure of his paintings, the banning of his works from public collections, and — the most awful measure in 1941 — his being banned from painting. Deeply injured, Nolde retired to his house where he secretly painted on scraps of paper with water colours, incunables of a distressed artist's soul. These were later to go down in history as "the unpainted pictures", disturbing examples of inhuman oppression and the tenacious resistance of a great personality.

Although the end of the war in 1945 also brought an end to Emil Nolde's ordeal, he was physically very weak and unable to get over the death of his wife in the following year: He began to convert his "unpainted pictures" into large oil paintings, but realized, "If I am to paint all of them, my lifetime will have to be more than doubled." For almost ten years, the brown dictators had hindered him in the completion of his artistic work.

The paintings on the following pages:

41
EMIL NOLDE
Anemonies and Amaryllis, undated
Aquarelle. 47 x 33.5 cm
Staatliche Graphische Sammlung, Munich

42
EMIL NOLDE
Tulips, undated
Aquarelle. 33.5 x 44 cm
Leopold Hoesch Museum, Düren

43
EMIL NOLDE
Dusk
Aquarelle. 35 x 45.5 cm
Kunstmuseum, Dusseldorf

44
EMIL NOLDE
Dahlias, Lilies, and Sunflowers
Aquarelle. 47.5 x 37.8 cm
Museum der Stadt Ulm

41

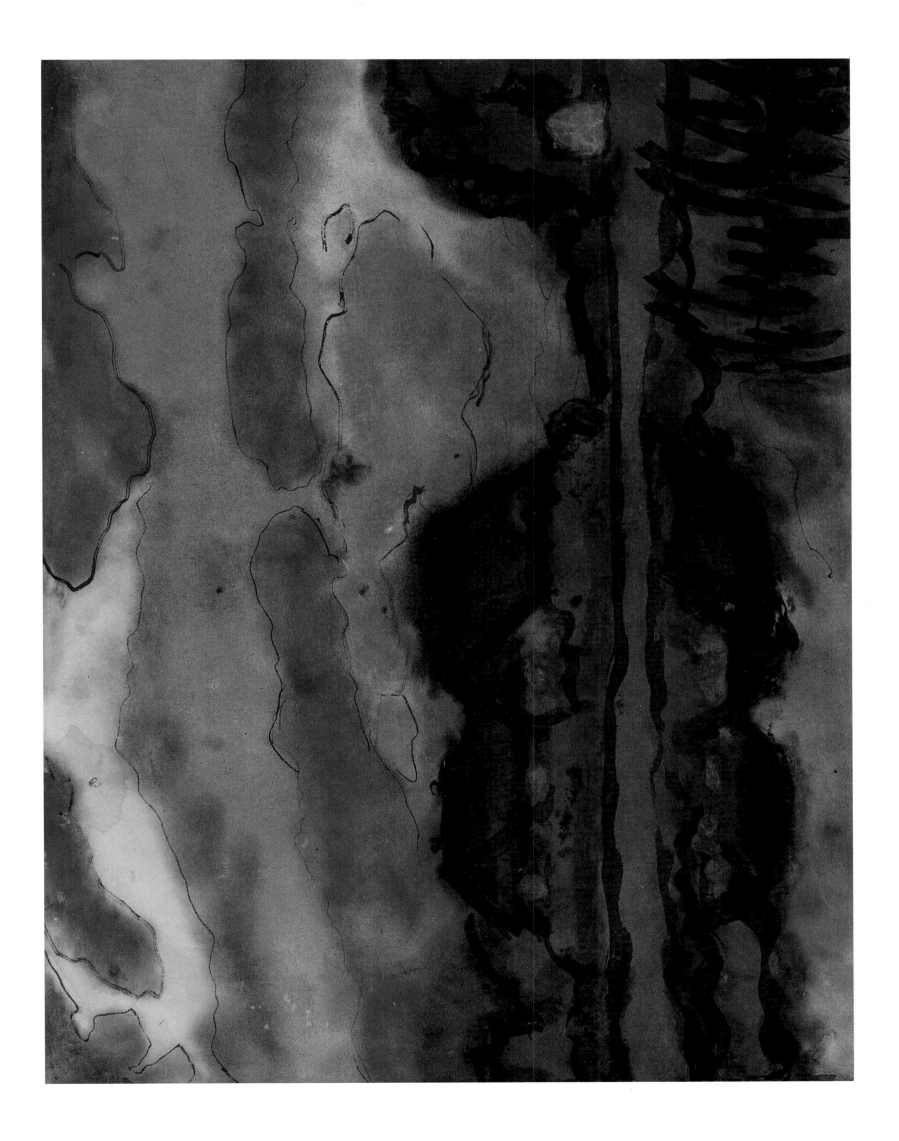

Lyonel Feininger
1871 New York — 1956 New York

"Feininger has created an art which stands on its own, unmistakable and incomparable, an art which could not find any adherents or imitators. Feininger has very little to do with real cubism which he is often related to: long before any cubist tendencies one can recognize a trend to a crystalline, polished design in his early works. A certain secret, tightly structured tetonic music lives in Feininger's art. It is therefore not surprising to find that his father was a violinist, his mother a singer, and that the son was on the way to studying music. As an artist he composed organ concertos of standing and remained lifelong a passionate player of Bach's music. This special musical element, however, gives Feininger's creations something detached from reality, something — sit venia verbo — abstract, although none of these creations would have been possible without direct analysis of the visual world, certainly a world which was highly individually and most ingeniously interpreted. It is the musicality which is the reason for Feininger's two picture themes: architecture of every size, epoch, and kind, sheds, churches, bridges, gabled houses, skyscrapers, and the sea with wide sweeping sand dunes next to it, with cloud structures and drifting steamboats and sailing ships." (Emil Pretorius)

Lyonel Feininger, born in New York, son of two artists who originated from Germany, came to Germany originally to train as a violinist. Several months before the start of his studies he was induced to visit a drawing course in the college of arts-and-crafts in Hamburg, yielding to an inclination which had always been present. This sudden decision was to have consequences which would influence his life; his talent was recognized, and he was admitted into the Berlin academy. A tendency and ability to caricature helped him in the following year to obtain commissions, and the proceeds from drawing cartoons enabled him to pay for his studies. The summer months in 1891 saw him as a well employed illustrator of humorous drawings on the island of Rügen. Here the unconstrained nature, the free play of the elements, and the unique atmosphere of sea, huddled villages, ships, and gnarled people deeply affected and encouraged him to work — now as a painter and graphic artist. A short trip to Paris widened his views on the trends of modern art, but could not captivate him decisively. Soon the young artist also found the drawing commissions of those years a form of drudgery, since they did not offer him any artistic perspective, whereas his serious graphic and painting attempts did not meet with any response in the meantime. A longer contract with the Chicago Tribune, for whom he took over two comic strip serials, gave him more pleasure, as he was allowed a free hand in what he did. Both serials, The Kin-der Kids and Wee Willie Winkie's World, are well acclaimed today by the intellectual public.

Feininger first found his way to painting and colour at the age of 36, motivated by a lengthy stay in Paris, where, in a circle of artists around Henri Matisse, artistic intentions were discussed daily. Without compromise he immediately began the composition of areas and structures, working from the colour, without clinging to the drawing skills which he had learnt during his long craft training. Works from van Gogh and Cézanne, but also the paintings of Turner, which he had seen on a trip to London, left a deep impression on him. In 1908 he returned to Berlin where he got married. He attempted to repress the drawing commissions so that he could concentrate more on painting. The paintings which are described as Feininger's figurative period were created, an abundance of interesting works which he was soon able to exhibit successfully in Paris as well as in Germany, due to his active contact with other progressive artists of the period. He got to know the artists' group Brücke, a circle which interested him a lot, although he was unable to share the same artistic opinions as Kirchner, Heckel, Schmidt-Rottluff, and Pechstein. The uncompromising, direct message made by these artists completely contradicted his sensitive style full of nuances. He was, however, drawn to the circle Der Blaue Reiter who gladly accepted him in their midst, and especially Paul Klee became a congenial friend.

Contact to the publisher Herwarth Walden and his "Sturm" was very important for another section of Feininger's work. The name "Sturm" originally belonged to an art magazine founded by Walden, but in 1912 a gallery was added which soon became the focus of avant-garde aspirations in the fine arts. In 1916, an art school was added. It was not just that two exhibitions for Feininger were organized which increased the circle of patrons and admirers, the artist also found the decisive impulse and stimulation for printing, especially woodcuts. He plunged into this new medium, over one hundred woodcuts were made alone in 1918.

A new intellectual life, closely connected with social ideas developed from the complete collapse after World War I. One of the most impressive deeds was the foundation of the Bauhaus by Walter Gropius who appointed Lyonel Feininger as his first master. In him he found a fellow combatant who remained true to the establishment until its liquidation by the National Socialists. He was deeply disturbed by the fateful political development which increasingly brought the force into power which had to fill any open-minded, liberal, active artist with horror. Feininger attempted to carry on his work although the political forces which increasingly interfered in his life hampered his artistic work. In 1937, he sadly left

Germany with his family and moved to New York which remained his home for the rest of his life.

"The years after his emigration were very difficult for Feininger. His art derived from a century old cultural tradition. His circle of friends in Germany were people who, like him, were bound up with a spiritual tradition. "Education" was not a catchword for him, he lived it, and of course it found a place in his art. His life in the New World plunged him into a crisis. The new surroundings paralysed him. It was not until the end of 1939, after a two years' break, that he found the strength for New York." (J. Schwarz)

Gradually the country became a theme. His love of ships helped him, and eventually the groups of houses and skyscrapers appeared in his work.

The main time for his work as an aquarellist was from 1924 until his emigration. With a very delicate combination of light sketching which only suggested the most necessary contours and a restrained use of colour he was able to create dreamlike, unmistakably original paintings, examples of his aristocratic sensitive artist's personality. Some of the elements from his aquarelles, for example the economic consideration of subdued lining in its connection with areas of colour, was carried over into his later oil paintings from America.

Like a transcription, Feininger showed the American people the beauty and attraction of their world in his paintings. He was able to achieve more and more recognition, whereby one has to take into account that, aged 66, he had to face completely new circumstances. America thanked him in that it awarded him increasingly more regard and honour, and within a few years made his birthplace his home again. But in Europe it was only possible after 1945 to bring his tremendous work close to the people again.

The paintings on the following pages:

49
LYONEL FEININGER
West-Deep, 1934
Aquarelle. 23.8 x 42 cm
Karl-Ernst-Osthaus Museum, Hagen

50/51
LYONEL FEININGER
Mönchroda, 1922
Aquarelle with quill drawing
Haags Gemeentemuseum, The Hague

52
LYONEL FEININGER
Vision of a Barque, 1935
Aquarelle. 30 x 41 cm
Kaiser Wilhelm Museum, Krefeld

49

oe/a   26. Dez. 1922

Ewald Mataré
1887 Aachen — 1965 Büderich near Dusseldorf

The artist Ewald Mataré began his career as a painter with an academic training. As the student of a history painter and later, with no convincing success, of Lovis Corinth, he was unable to find the creative power to free himself of the old-fashioned ideas which he had acquired in the academy. Although he was a perfect painter from a craftsman's point of view, the step needed to become an individual and assertive artist was denied to him at first.

He achieved his artistic perfection in a roundabout way: his strong partiality for the sea made him visit Northern beaches for his leisure as well as for painting. Driftwood excited his imagination and encouraged him to make sculptures from organic wooden structures. This became the turning point. Once he was sure of his future course, Mataré retired every year from spring till autumn to the coast of Estonia or Finland where he worked exclusively in wood. In this way, the long series of intimate animal sculptures was developed which represent his very own contribution to the history of modern art and which rightly establish his international standing. The quality of his free sculptures soon helped him to receive commissions for applied art, stained glass windows, reliefs, and mosaics. In 1932, he received a professorship in the sculpture class in Dusseldorf through the engagement of Dr. Kaesbach who had already brought Paul Klee there from Dessau. This appointment, however, did not last very long. In the following year, the Nazis forced his dismissal. Dr. Kaesbach lost his post, Paul Klee moved back to Switzerland. Mataré's works were removed from the museums as ''degenerate'' and were sold cheaply. Friends in the clergy of the Catholic Church helped the artist in the following difficult years with commissions in the sacral field. He was not under observation to any great extent so that he was at least able to continue his work with his animal figures and wood carvings in his private studio. After the end of the war he was made provisional head of the Dusseldorf academy, but as he was unable to enforce his reformative ideas which seemed necessary to him, he withdrew from the academy again soon afterwards.

The aquarelle stands completely separate from Mataré's other works. ''First I go back to nature and then I begin to abstract,'' he once wrote. An economic, diffused use of colour discloses the structures. Basically, the paintings are little meditations, a sinking into nature. A year before his death Mataré wrote, ''I do not want to take on any new work now, and if I can just have a break, perhaps a month somewhere in the country, I would like to bring the aquarelle to a higher level, with a new internal impetus. Dürer hard on my heels! He painted some trees — I am left breathless!''

Piet Mondriaan
1872 Amersfort — 1944 New York

The fact that the master of the Dutch constructivists, one of the founders and the strongest defender of abstract art, was in his early work, the creator of naturalistic landscape aquarelles may astound. It is, on the other hand, certainly an indication of the high masterly skills of the artist.

Mondriaan came from an active artistic family. His uncle was a painter, and his father also painted, though not professionally. The young Piet received his first basic training from his uncle until, aged 20, he was accepted by the Rijksakademie in Amsterdam. Because of his art studies there, he came in contact with the artists from Barbizon. A studious young person absorbs a lot, and Mondriaan did not remain indifferent to his contact with the Impressionists. With the same amount of interest, he took in the paintings of the Fauves, but everything just as impressions, in passing, so to speak. He was just as little a follower of the Impressionists as he was a form-breaking expressionist. As Jan Toorop was one of his tutors, there was even a certain contact with art nouveau, certainly a basis for his way of seeing things graphically.

His astounding development began around 1910 with the frame-filling painting of a fruit tree. This tree remained his favourite theme for a long time. He continuously gave it new forms in new paintings. He made it abstract in colours and in form, in oil paintings and in sketches, until the tree became a type of structure, a geometrical framework. Then he used the same procedure with other forms, he abstracted in stages and divided his construction into cubist areas. From 1914 onwards, he went away from any kind of representation, he did not give his paintings any titles which would remind one of the initial form in nature, but rather carried the abstraction consequently further and gave his paintings titles such as "Composition No. 7". A few years later, he began the long series of well-balanced constructions which were to bring him renown: rectangles of colour which were balanced by lines, likewise running at right angles.

Mondriaan described his method, "I discarded the natural colours in favour of pure colours. I had come to the conclusion that one cannot reproduce the colours of nature on canvas. I felt instinctively that art had to find a new path to put the beauty of nature across." And several years later, "The means of expression are always those of shape and colour though in their most complete spiritualization; the straight line and the pure colour remain pure artistic methods of expression. In spite of all differentiation of expression, every art form, whichever it may be, will eventually become with the progressing culture of the spirit an exact presentation of balanced relations."

Oskar Schlemmer
1888 Stuttgart — 1943 Baden-Baden

The fundamental change to new spiritual ideas which moved Germany's intellectuals after the complete downfall at the end of World War I was responsible for the emergence of reformed spiritual, artistic, and craft training centres in many places. One of the most successful establishments, rationally thought out in its foundation and efficiently run, was the Bauhaus in Weimar, which was founded and built by Walter Gropius. It came about with the union of the art academy and the college of arts-and-crafts. Gropius replaced the familiar academic classes with modern working groups, where the artists, committed to the mediaeval thoughts of the masonic lodge, should be trained and taught with a common aim in mind under the leadership of the architects. An alien element in the small town administration, considered anti-reactionary and troublesome by the rising Third Reich, the Bauhaus did not have a good standing in the country from the beginning. It was obvious that the National Socialists would not waste any time after their takeover in dissolving this liberal, intellectual, and artistic establishment. The significance of the Bauhaus in relation to modern art is obvious when one makes a short list of the tutors. It resembles an encyclopaedia of modern art: Klee, Feininger, Kandinsky, Moholy-Nagy, Marcks, Itten, and many more. One of them, a central figure, was Oskar Schlemmer. Along with Feininger he was a main style-forming representative.

Oskar Schlemmer was a pupil of Adolf Hölzel in Stuttgart. In his work this important painter went through several changes of style which were logically obtained from the previous one. One of the main characteristics was his ability to transmit to his pupils what he himself had worked out in the consequent execution of his art. No other tutor outside the Bauhaus had such an enduring influence on modern art in Germany as Hölzel. His artistic precept stimulated a series of great artists with an incredibly varied stylistic spectrum. Schlemmer also took the educational behaviour pattern from this tutor with him into the international association of the Bauhaus.

Schlemmer's artistic work is complex, the aquarelle contributes a small, but intimate and technically interesting part. The double ability of painter and sculptor which is relatively seldom was supplemented by stage decorations, large murals, and reliefs. Also a successful "Triadic Ballet" created by him belongs to his works. It brings his strictly formed and at the same time audacious figures onto the stage.

The paintings on the following pages:

57
EWALD MATARÉ
Riverbanks on the Rhine, around 1930
Aquarelle on pencil. 24.5 x 91 cm
Private collection

58/59
PIET MONDRIAAN
Landscape with Water Trench, around 1906
Aquarelle, mix technique
Haags Gemeentemuseum, The Hague

60
OSKAR SCHLEMMER
Girl's Head in Vertical Stripes, 1932
Aquarelle. 28 x 22 cm
Staatsgalerie Stuttgart

59

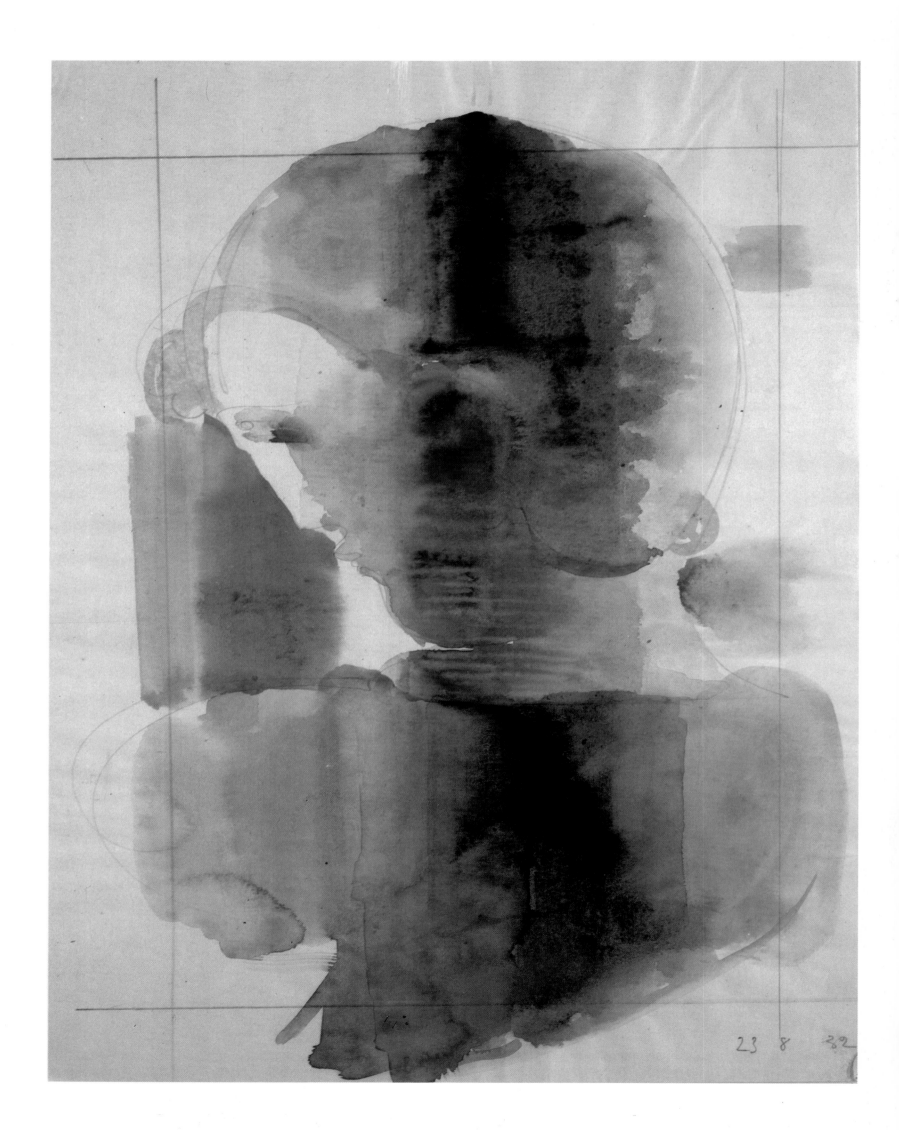

23 8 82

60

Heribert Losert
1913 Neukirchen — lives in Wörth a. d. Donau

There are very few present-day artists who devote themselves so actively to aquarelle painting as Heribert Losert does. He recognized early how much the special transparency of this technique suits his artistic tendencies, which seem to be indebted to Klee's words, "Art does not reproduce visible things, but it makes things visible."

Losert, trained in the college of arts-and-crafts and in the academy of fine arts in Vienna, had to struggle to find spare time for his artistic activities while serving as a soldier from 1939 till 1945. This was mostly possible just with crayons. He was first able to detach himself from the troubles of the time to obtain some peace for his creative works at the start of the fifties; at that time the artistic medium necessary to realize his intentions was already completely present, well prepared with his previous graphic work. Style and means of expression were found in a very short time, an inspiring weightlessness is alive in all his works. Paul Rausch, an early biographer, writes about one of his first paintings, "Losert had found his personal form when this aquarelle was painted. This is most important for the artist of today where general compulsory contents do not exist any more, and where every artist tries to find his own way of expressing what he has to say. Beautiful, poetical pictures are thus gained, in an attractive way, mysterious images, paintings of an enchanted, dreamlike material world. Losert has painted such pictures ... Although the material world was important to him, as something which makes the secret of the world visible. Objects are not the sense and purpose in his paintings. His artistic efforts are the "spiritual" and "objective". And how would it be otherwise possible to represent these than 'under the picture' of forms."

The inner need to convey a suitable human relationship to art and to make clear the necessity of an artistic activity as the prerequisite for the achievement of a well balanced life for everyone, occasioned Losert to take on teaching assignments in different Waldorf schools between 1953 and 1961. He also worked as a lecturer in the study centre of free art in Ottersberg, and eventually gave annual art courses as an introduction into art. "Heribert Losert's art is of a high technical ability, and as surely and masterly as he commands his medium, he never lapses into virtuosity. His sensitivity and transparency are meant as an immense and unchanging call to humanity. For him art is never just a means of edification or pretty aesthetic play, more a healing factor in view of the threat to human nature in our time, in fact to humanity itself." (Ernst Schremmer)

Paul Klee
1879 Münchenbuchsee near Bern — 1940 Muralto near Locarno

Paul Klee had a considerable influence on the development of modern art which remains as strong as ever in the present day, in fact increasingly so. At the same time, his work goes beyond any scope if one was to try to classify it in any direction of style or genre. His work in aquarelle painting also is in accordance with this versatility: water-colours were always a favourite and constantly used medium. But hardly any painter has used them in so many different ways, mix techniques, and varieties as Paul Klee. Hans Hess tells of an entry of Paul Klee's one evening in the famous visitors' book of the Hess house, "Paul Klee brought his little sieves and spraying equipment with him and blew and rubbed the picture on the desk. Water colour, ink, and paintbrush were always in the house …"

Paul Klee's father was a music teacher. Paul played the violin excellently, he remained close to the instrument and to music for the whole of his life. A lot has drifted into his painting which had its origin in melody or rhythmic construction. Klee began his studies in Munich where he became a pupil of the great Franz von Stuck; this connection appears to us slightly bewildering in retrospect, "to be a pupil of Stuck," Klee once said, "had a good ring to it. In reality, it wasn't half as magnificent. I made no headway with colour. As the emotional tone played a major part in my command of form, I attempted to profit at least here as much as possible. And with Stuck, there really was a lot to learn in that respect …

In 1906, Klee married the pianist Lily Stumpf and moved to Munich. Leopold Zahn described his studio in the Wernecksschlößchen in Schwabing, "A noble mourning of decay hung over the house and grounds. Goats grazed on the grass under ancient trees. The foresaken land-house with the walled in grounds, away from the city and bustlinc people, suited him completely. It seemed to be necessary for him to isolate himself, to live on his own in a world where everyday life was a fleeting reflex. I never had the feeling that I was close to Klee. He never appeared completely present, or completely of this world to me … Emil Nolde once called him a 'butterfly in a starry sky'. At the same time his lifestyle was middleclass, remote from a bohemian picturesque anarchy."

Klee joined the group around Der Blaue Reiter and began to involve himself with problems of colour. In this respect, he occupied himself with Delauney, whose essay "On the Subject of Light" he had translated for the magazine "Der Sturm". His legendary trip to Tunis, which also changed the attitude of his travelling companions, Macke and Moilliet, to colour brought the artist great revelations. He discovered the intrinsic value of colour and was able to further develop Delauney's ideas in his work. In 1914, Klee wrote these lines in his diary which have become famous. "It presses into me deep and mild, I feel this and become so sure, without taking great pains. The colour possesses me. I don't have to pursue it. It has got me forever, I know it. That is the revelation of this blessed moment: I and the colour are as one. I am an painter."

In 1920, Walter Gropius brought the painter to the Bauhaus as a tutor. This was a happy and creative time for Klee. Working closely together with his colleagues brought a lot of stimulation, and the relation to Kandinsky was especially fruitful. Kandinsky, Feininger, Jawlensky, and Klee formed the group "Die Blauen Vier"; the great papers on theories of art were published: The "Pedagogic Sketchbook" which conveyed the basis of his teaching and "Pictorial Thinking". An intellectual acuteness as well as a constructivistic thoroughness, which one would not have suspected in such a basically romantic artist, were revealed in these papers. Klee, too, drifted away from the representation of nature. "The painting does not want to represent a section of nature seen through a window, but rather wants to show its own reality: that of the picture. The urge to get to the bottom of appearances and to bring hidden layers into vision broke through. The novelty with Klee is that he incorporated the whole periphery of experience and of ideas into a plastic presentation and thus created an undreamt of enrichment and enlargement of the means of expression of his own world, of his 'world interior'. But what does it bring to light? Memories and experiences of the internal and external world. He brings to the forefront that intermediate stage which was almost buried since the Enlightment: gentle, lyrical visions and playful magic, threatening signs and curious ideas, foreign hieroglyphs and mystic ciphers. Klee's individuality lies in the subtle, almost somnambulent perception. Thus a phenomenon such as Klee could only unfold and flourish in this thinned and partly esoteric climate. With Klee, the spirit of German romanticism was revived. Irony is also added, regulating and keeping a distance. Two basic forms determine his picture world: naivety and creative detachment, both held together by an imperturbable innocence." (Fritz Nemitz)

In 1931, Paul Klee took a professorship in the Dusseldorf academy after the tense situation in the Bauhaus had increasingly oppressed and hindered his work in the years before the National Socialists came to power. Leaving his friends from the Bauhaus behind was difficult for him. At that time, the Dusseldorf academy was regarded as the best in Germany and Klee could fully concentrate on his painting courses. But in 1933 he was dismissed together with all the other progressive tutors: Klee returned to Bern from the country which he was deeply rooted in, forced out by the Nazis. In his last 3 years he painted — already fatally ill — his most impressive metaphors, imprinted by the approaching times of terror.

The paintings on the following pages:

65
HERIBERT LOSERT
Opposite, 1982
Aquarelle. 42 × 60 cm
In the artist's collection

66/67
HERIBERT LOSERT
Dolls, 1958
Aquarelle. 43 × 61 cm
Private collection

68
PAUL KLEE
Mountains in Winter, 1925
Aquarelle, sprayed on paper grounded with chalk. 28.7 × 37 cm
Paul-Klee-Stiftung, Kunstmuseum Bern
Hermann und Margrit Rupf-Stiftung

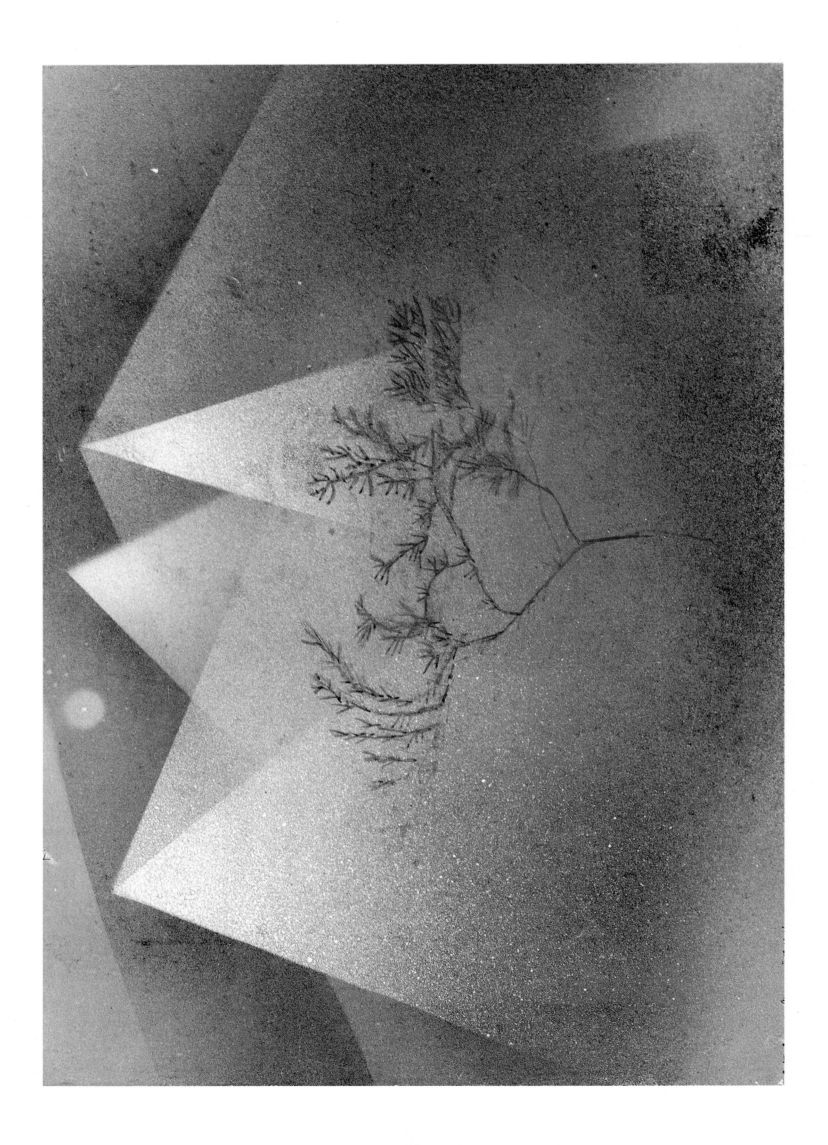

68

Franz Marc

1880 Munich — 1916 near Verdun

The normal problems of form in painting were not the starting point of Franz Marc's considerations. He was involved with the "original basis" of artistic creation from which, according to him, the solutions had to come or at least had to be sensed. "Is there, for the artist, a more mysterious idea than imagining how an animal sees nature? How does a horse see the world? Or an eagle, a deer, or a dog? How sad and soulless our conventions are to put animals in a landscape which belongs to our eyes rather than immerse ourselves in the soul of the animal and guess its visual range ... Art will free itself from human application and human wishes. We will not paint the forest or the horse the way we want to or the way they appear to us, but how they really are, how the forest or the horse itself feels, their absolute being which lives behind the appearance which we see." It was not the external impression as seen by the Impressionists, not the expressionistic wish to make internal impressions visible which were the aims of Marc's art. He wanted to get to know the nature of the represented animal and to place it into the world which was appropriate to it.

We can already anticipate from Marc's early work how well he understood the internal forces of nature, but the proper access to colour was still missing. His friend August Macke, who he was bound up with through communal work, had at this time an unconstrained attitude towards colour, but unfortunately could not show him the way decisively. The triggering impulse came with an exhibition of the Neue Künstlervereinigung, seeing the paintings by Wassilij Kandinsky and Alexej Jawlensky. The Russian-Slavic pleasure in strong accent was expressed in extraordinary colourfulness. The obstacle was removed like an open floodgate, and suddenly Marc knew what had been missing, "Everything had an organic basis for me, apart from the colour." He plunged into this new area of work. Unrelentingly, he occupied himself with his very personal system of complementary colours in order to lay aside, as he said, his "arbitrary choice of colours." "I feel that I have more success every day," he wrote in a letter from those days, "I am also glad that I am able to do it in such seclusion, without colleagues etc., surely I get something more individual and original out of it, the same as it used to be with my compositions and ideas of colour. The latter are truly over and done with. A step backwards would be completely impossible..."

And really, his painting of the three red horses from 1910/11 is a breakthrough within his own creativity as well as to the outside — a confirmation of his troublesome search. In quick succession there followed a whole series of animal paintings, incomparable and unmistakable in their way of putting a message across. "An Eros of Franciscan power of love is combined with the emotional understanding of the devine purity of the creature. He removed from the animals all the details, everything conditional and accidental of their empirical appearance and summarized the wealth of their being in a gesture which grasps the senses directly. He raised them above the border line of natural reality into the spiritual area of imagination." (H. Bünemann)

The colour became a signal effect for the symbolic content and did not have a function for a naturalistic representation. Colour and object were treated as unconnected elements in the painting, whereby the colour of course followed a certain set of rules. Blue stood for the male aspect, austerety and intellect, yellow for the female aspect, softness, cheerfulness, and sensuousness, and red embodied matter. "Every colour has to say clearly who and what it is and has to have a clear form." Marc explained, ". . . I would never make a bush blue just for a decorative effect, but only to increase the personality of the horse which stands out from it. But the media always have to be purely artistic."

With all the struggle about the spiritualness in art, about painting being a properly recognized higher insight, Franz Marc lived in an era in occidental history which was full of vigour. It was a time of change not only for art but for life as a whole. His intellectual awareness forced him to take part in the hustle and bustle, to see the trends, and declare his stand. It is therefore not surprising that he was soon at the centre of a group of artists who recognized new concepts and who attempted to show them to the world with force. At the same time the struggle with artistic problems was an integral part of his personality. Here he attempted to work in solitude and peace. Helmuth Macke, who lived and worked with Marc for several months in Sindelshof, tells us about the concentration on his work, "Marc lived a very regulated life. At half past eight, after breakfast, he was in his studio, or rather his loft, and painted till the church bell rang twelve o'clock, at which time the big white Alsatian also began to howl. Half past one at the latest, Marc stood in front of his easel again, in the draughty loft with unplastered roof-tiles where the temperature was much the same as outside. He was wrapped in an old black coat with the astrakhan collar turned up. He was completely absorbed in his work since at this time he found the breakthrough to his own form. He always worked on a series of paintings at once. In the afternoon, Marc worked until it got dark, and after dinner he sat in his cane chair, drawing and ruminating, and at that time most of the ideas for his pictures came about."

The same man was active in the art scene in Munich, encouraged others unremittingly, had a large circle of artist friends, struggled for exhibitions, concerned himself with the daily politics of artists' organizations, in short, he took a lively interest in day to day life. Although he lived under difficult circumstances, financially and in his private life, he found the opportunity to bring out with vehemence the almanac Der Blaue Reiter, an ambitious project which he realized together with Kandinsky. The editorial office became the meeting-place for the elite of Munich painters. Marc's flat in Schwabing, the artists' quarter in Munich, was the central meeting and debating place in those years for a considerable number of those people who were the leading personalities in 20th century art.

Franz Marc was also the driving force behind the exhibitions from editors of Der Blaue Reiter. The first one took place in 1911 in the Thannhausser gallery, a second one at Goltz. The second exhibition was dedicated to graphics and had, apart from several young French artists, many works from the Brücke artists. Especially the printed graphics with their completely new form by Kirchner, Heckel, and Schmidt-Rotluff evoked interest in Marc and the other Munich artists, as they were still a long way from being able to unfold themselves so freely.

One can see from many letters how much work (desk work this time), how many discussions and considerations had to be invested in the publication of the almanac. But he was overcome with satisfaction when the work was eventually finished. "I had such a feeling of happiness to see it before me at last", Marc wrote to Kandinsky, "I am also sure of one thing: Many silent people in this country and many young forces will secretly be grateful to us, be inspired by the book, and compare their world to it; perhaps the book and the ensuing volumes could become a code of law for our disrupted times. I often think about the second volume and already have my ideas on it; I am thinking about a long contribution with a lot of illustrations as a way of expressing the very personal "years of learning" which I am going through at the moment."

The paintings on the following pages:

73
FRANZ MARC
Fabulous Creatures (Horse and Dog), 1913
Aquarelle on pencil sketch.
44 × 36.3 cm
Graphische Sammlung der Staatsgalerie, Stuttgart

74/75
FRANZ MARC
Three Horses at the Trough
(Three Horses at a Stream in the Forest), 1913/14
Tempera. 39.7 × 45.5 cm
Staatliche Kunsthalle, Karlsruhe

76
FRANZ MARC
Lying Bull, 1913
Tempera. 40 × 46 cm
Museum Folkwang, Essen

August Macke
1887 Meschede — 1914 near Perthes-les Hurlus

August Macke was no rebel and not disposed to fighting. He was a sensuous person, an instinctive painter with a well-balanced harmonious nature, such as one seldom finds in German art. "I am working terribly hard just now," he wrote, "that means, work is for me the happiness of nature, the glowing sun, and the trees, bushes, people, animals . . . I become engrossed in the nodding of the snowdrop, in the rhythm of the branches full of birds, swinging in the sun, in the magnificent jumping and creeping of our cat, in the sedate smile of red-cheeked apples . . ."

Macke grew up in Cologne and Bonn and attended the Düsseldorf academy while still quite young. He soon moved to the school of arts-and-crafts where the more varied tuition appeared more important to him. He also received his first commissions through the change. Louise Dumont, who was head of the theatre at the time, noticed him and asked him to design stage decorations and costumes; an incredible assignment for an art student who was not yet 20 years old. As an eye-minded person he was especially receptive to impressions gained while travelling and always strived after possibilities to travel. He made his first journey to Italy in 1905 with his friends Walter and Elisabeth Gerhardt (Elisabeth Gerhardt was to become his wife in 1909), in the following year he saw Holland, Belgium, and, for a short time, London. There followed trips to Paris, six months in Berlin, where he was a pupil of Lovis Corinth, and in 1908 again Italy and Paris. Military service brought a one year interruption in his study trips, but he was already travelling again in the year of his marriage, to Frankfurt, Colmar, and Switzerland, then to Paris.

He got to know Franz Marc in 1909; this was to have a decisive meaning for his art. Both artists were able to learn from the personality and ability of the other: Macke had a freer approach to colour. Marc, on the other hand, was soon able to convince his friend that a valid piece of art needed an intensity of thought. Being together helped both artists considerably. Another artist was very important for Macke's training with his views about colour. The Frenchman Robert Delauney delivered the components for Macke's picture compositions with the unity and opposition of pure areas of colour.

In 1912, Macke and Marc travelled to Paris. They visited Delauney, the open-minded artist, whose cheerful attitude was similar to that of the German Macke.

A close friendship developed between Delauney and Macke. Thanks to Macke's influence, the first Delauney exhibition was able to be held in Cologne.

It is worth mentioning another journey, a trip which only lasted two weeks and which went down in history as the Journey to Cairuan. August Macke travelled together with Louis Moilliet and Paul Klee to Tunis. The few days in the African countryside in spring were filled with an almost intoxicated production. Macke produced 38 aquarelles and a great number of drawings and sketches. The aquarelles became a document of a newly reached stage in maturity. The transparent floating water colours, painted with a light hand, join together to form a distinct harmony without any impurity. The long sought "ecstasy of colour" — Macke achieved it here. The other two artists also found the way to new and convincing work on this trip so that these few days go down as one of the great moments in the development of modern art.

The almanac Der Blaue Reiter which had been published by Marc and Kandinsky also contained a picture from Macke which was well received. Macke had followed the preparatory work and consideration for this almanac with some interest and had done some work on it, but he had kept a certain critical distance from the art-political activities of his friends. With all his tendency to passionate commitment, he recognized that the constant documentations and explanations of his friend and Kandinsky's attempts to understand "the intellectuality in art" led away from the artistic world as he saw it. But he was always a willing partner to Marc with considerations and discussions about the meaning and use of colour. He later wrote to him from Bonn about his new discoveries, "What I have found new in painting is as follows: There are certain harmonies of colour if you like, a certain red and green which flutter when you look at them. Now, if you put a tree in a landscape you can either look at the tree or the landscape because of the stereoscopic effect. If you now paint something three-dimensional, the coloured timbre which flutters is a three-dimensional colour effect, and if you paint a landscape and the green leaves flutter a little with the translucent blue sky, that is because the green is evident in nature on a different level from the sky. Our noble aim is to find this stereoscopic energy of colour instead of being satisfied with a lifeless clair-obscure."

August Macke only had eight years to practise his art, eight years from the beginning of his recognized activity as an artist till his death in World War I. Franz Marc wrote in his moving obituary, "One of the most beautiful and courageous curves in our German artistic development is abruptly snapped off with the death of August Macke; none of us are able to continue with it. We artists know well that with the elimination of his harmonies, colour in German art will fade by several shades and will have a duller, drier timbre. He gave colour a brighter and purer ring than any of us, so clear and bright as his whole personality was."

Wassilij Kandinsky
1866 Moscow — 1944 Paris

He was thirty years old, a respected ethnologist and artistic editor in a large printers, doctor of law, and a successful businessman, when he decided to go to Germany to study art. It appeared a relatively unprofitable study compared to an established middle-class existence. The determining factor for his decision is supposed to have been an exhibition of French Impressionists in St. Petersburg. As if in a sudden enlightenment, he understood the meaning of the complete detachment of colour and painting from the subject. Kandinsky went to Munich to train as an artist. His tutor was Franz von Stuck. In the initial years he fell under the spell of art nouveau which at that time was very powerful and prevailing in Munich. He painted charming fairy-tale pictures, examples of his ingenious talent. A fellow student was his Russian compatriot Alexej Jawlensky who was later to become a companion and friend. Art nouveau paintings which were completely motivated by his Russian homeland followed, then impressionistic landscapes, and soon paintings with the unrestricted colour of the Fauves. After many years of travel, Kandinsky moved in 1908 together with the artist Gabriele Münter to Murnau in the forelands of the Bavarian Alps. Soon his colleagues Jawlensky and Marianne von Werefkin joined him. Naturally, he had contact with Franz Marc, with whom he later formed an inspiring working team and who also became a good friend. Together they planned and worked on the publication of the almanac 'Der Blaue Reiter'. They also used this name for their activities of organizing exhibitions.

The central problem, though, which occupied Kandinsky was the abandoning of the object, turning to a picture of form and colour — deliberately leaving out the object — to an abstract picture as an expression of pure composition. This searching eventually found its first manifestation in 1910: Kandinsky painted his first abstract aquarelle which was followed by an oil painting in 1911. Now he had found the key, and his experimentation and contemplation found expression in paintings as well as in writings, which retained his trains of thought. In 1912, his theories appeared in print for the first time, ''On the Spirituality in Art''.

In the following years of World War I and World War II, he had to move several times. First his return to Russia was inevitable, then he was able to move to the Bauhaus in Weimar, and in 1933, he had to emigrate to France. He untiringly expanded on his works on the theory of art, which he supported with a great number of impressive paintings, till he died.

The paintings on the following pages:

81
AUGUST MACKE
Interior of the Country-House in St. Germain, 1914
Tunis-Aquarelle. 26 × 21 cm
Städtisches Kunstmuseum, Bern

82/83
AUGUST MACKE
With a Yellow Jacket, 1913
Aquarelle. 29.5 × 44.5 cm
Museum der Stadt Ulm

84
WASSILIJ KANDINSKY
Composition, 1921
Aquarelle. 30.4 × 47.1 cm
Karl-Ernst-Osthaus-Museum, Hagen

Christian Rohlfs
1849 Niendorf — 1938 Hagen

Christian Rohlfs is one of those artists for whom the aquarelle has a special meaning, in fact it is the part of his work which has brought the artist world renown. He was fifty years old, when he found this liberated style which is displayed in his great paintings. He only found his form at this age, and a truly impressive collection of late works was created, unique in many ways. He was incredibly prolific; in the year before his death, at the age of 86, he painted 137 aquarelles each of which is more magnificent in colourfulness and perfection than the next.

But it is not just the advanced age in connection with the achievement of absolute mastership which is unusual in the life of Christian Rohlfs: his way to art is also remarkable. He was born, the son of a farmer, in the wide open countryside near the border to Denmark. Nothing was further from his parents' minds than their son becoming an artist. When he was 15, he had an accident which left him an invalid and made him unsuitable for farming. The doctor who treated the young boy recognized his artistic talents, persuaded the parents to allow him to attend the secondary school, and finally drew his brother-in-law's attention to him — the writer Theodor Storm. He was actually able to help him to be accepted in the academy in Weimar, and so a highly original artist was given his start. Rohlfs proved to be a good pupil, detached himself, however, from the common academy style, hardly took part in exhibitions, and began to go his own way, as much as this was possible along with his studies.

He tended towards working in the open and arrived through his own discernment at an impressionistic form of colour and light, even before the detailed knowledge of the new style had reached Weimar from France. In 1898/99 Rohlfs first displayed his impressionistic paintings publicly. The exhibition was a success, and an intensive process of learning led to a respected artistry. At this turning point, the personality of Karl-Ernst Osthaus and Henry van de Velde were of decisive importance for him. As Maecenas, Osthaus did not only want to build a museum for modern art in his home town, but also wanted to combine this with an artists' colony, the Folkwangschule. Van de Velde recommended Rohlfs who received the honourable invitation to work in this art school. His reputation was now established, and in 1902 it was crowned with the bestowal of a professorship from the Weimar art academy.

Rohlfs style now became further and further removed from Impressionism: "Inspired by the profound work of Munch and the strong colourfulness of van Gogh, Rohlfs detaches himself from the loose elegance and sheer colour appeal of the pointillist manner and seeks a deepening of the colours, whereby he comes close to the intuition of expressionism. Although he does not paint a single pointillist picture in 1904, the technique is still obvious in some of his paintings. However, in his aquarelles a wide brushstroke and strong colour provide for a generous, concise, emphatic reproduction of reality. And soon his oil paintings also take on the flourishing, strong characteristics. The paint does not capture impressionistic moods any more, it is used in areas and becomes convincing, suggestive, and effectful. Rohlfs' paintings now resemble the early works of Kirchner and Heckel. With his change of style he becomes very prolific." (H. Froning)

1910 brought a positive change for the artist's hampering financial situation, but this went along with a deterioration of his artistic development. The collector Dr. Commerell invited Rohlfs to Bavaria and gave him 6000 Marks per annum for two years with the provision that all paintings which were made during this time belonged to him. As none of the honours conferred on the artist had ever brought him permanent employment or financial endowment, he was very glad about the prospect of a steady income. He moved to Ammerland and later to Erwald near the Zugspitze. Unfortunately, this tract proved to be a handicap for Rohlfs who came from the North. He could not feel at home in the sloping mountains under the glaring blue sky of the Bavarian countryside. He missed the mellow landscape with the diffused intermediate tones of the Westphalian air and the homelike architecture of this ancient cultural land. His reaction was inner insecurity which had an adverse effect on his work. The war also paralysed his creativeness, but brought as a spiritual retort the introversion which resulted in works full of religious themes. Bible scenes were represented in woodcuts, oil-paintings, and aquarelles. In these works, a deep inward engagement is obvious apart from great artistic maturity.

"After the war, flower paintings become more frequent again. As impressions of a wonderful play of colour, they represent growing, flowering, and wilting, not as a symbol for the rhythm of life but as purposeless, amusing plays of colour and form which give the moment durability." (H. Froning)

Christian Rohlfs had a very specific way of observing and painting. Hans Hess wrote appropriate words about his guest in his house in Erfurt, "The honourable but very amusing Christian Rohlfs visited us and painted Erfurt cathedral in fourteen versions like Monet had painted the cathedral of Rouen. When one observed how Rohlfs painted a city, a landscape, or a flower, one was able to understand how the artist uses his eyes as a tool of the intellect. In Ascona, he would sit for days on his terrace overlooking the lake, hardly saying anything, but with a look which absorbed and processed everything which he could see in nature." He appeared to gather impressions, so to speak, in order to reproduce them at another time in another place.

In spite of the qualified recognition in the art world, he suffered under the ignorance of the general public. The public first became aware of him in a positive light in 1918 on the occasion of a large exhibition in Frankfurt. Suddenly, it seems unbelievable that the sixty-eight year old could have remained "undiscovered" for so long and that he could have created this enormous collection of work unperturbed, without any noticeable reaction from the public. But Rohlfs did not stagnate even at this point. His really happy time now began. In 1919, he married Helene Vogt and with this new situation in his life, he found a new impetus. Full of energy, he absorbed himself in work, in his woodcuts and in the more essential elaboration of his aquarelle painting.

At the beginning of the 1930s, his health forced a stay in the South, something which he had always resisted in spite of medical advice, because he was afraid of a negative influence on his work. Rohlfs went to Ascona and realized that the flowing hills and the warm subdued light completely suited his artistic intentions, not as in Bavaria where the rugged mountains, the blue sky, and crystal clear atmosphere had disturbed him. Till his death, he spent nine months each year on Lake Maggiore.

He was always very interested in aquarelle painting. It should be pointed out that Rohlfs hardly ever made pure aquarelles. It was as with his graphic printing where he left a lot of room for experiment. He preferred tempera paints which, compared to aquarelle paints, have a greater density, but which, if thinned down enough, become transparent. He used these paints with various additives, on top of this he often worked with a dry paintbrush and a hard scrubbing brush. With this he removed a major part of the colour from large sections of the painting, whereby the rudiments of the colour remained and gave the roughed-up paper the patina of century old house walls.

The paintings on the following pages:

89
CHRISTIAN ROHLFS
Large Canna indica, 1935
Tempera. 79 × 58 cm
Museum Folkwang, Essen

90/91
CHRISTIAN ROHLFS
Poppy in a Vase, 1919
Aquarelle. 48 × 67 cm
Karl-Ernst-Osthaus-Museum, Hagen

92
CHRISTIAN ROHLFS
White Roses (Marschall Niels), 1920
Aquarelle (Mix Technique). 53 × 43 cm
Karl-Ernst-Osthaus-Museum, Hagen

Vincent van Gogh
1853 Zundert — 1890 Auvers

Our century is a time of changing analysis of the genius of van Gogh: a first generation of artists discovered the painter and found in his work the decisive steps in the fundamental change to modernism, which enabled those who followed to progress in their art. A second generation stood, deeply stirred, in the face of his immense work and the tragic background of his life, while a third generation now recognizes that the nature and work of the artist go beyond art and expand the borders of consciousness.

"Since these pictures were painted, mankind has suffered shocks and changes such as no other epoch has before. They have altered our inner selves. And from this transformation of our consciousness we recognize in Vincent van Gogh someone who has already suffered, alone, in unbounded loneliness, what has become for us the destiny of the age. The bourgeois world which meant stability and security in the 19th century has finally fallen apart. Van Gogh suspected the approaching end of this world and in pain created works in which a new view of life is announced which wants to make its way. He painted the moving wheels of the sun, golden waving fields, cypress trees which seem to be detached from the earth, but they are fought for and suffered for through years of loneliness; through days and nights of hunger and misery; through hours of deepest dispair. His paintings are like stations on the Roads of Passion. When we pass them, we can guess the suffering behind them, and the ways of someone who had to wrest his life's work from a sick body. The first paintings still carry the burdensome weight of the earth, opaque black-grey tones. The last creations, the sunflowers and landscapes from Provence, tell a story of the victory of light." (H. Feddersen)

Vincent van Gogh came from a distinguished Dutch Protestant family which had produced several clergymen. Van Gogh's father was a vicar himself. This background had a considerable influence on van Gogh's personality and struggles, in other respects it was also the fact that his uncle was an art dealer. He smoothed the way for the young Vincent's entry into an important art dealers for whom he worked in The Hague, London, and Paris. In this way, he saw many works of art which had a deep lasting effect on him. But since his work was more in the business side, it soon bored him. His interests tended more and more towards religion. He started to study theology in several different ways, failed, and eventually went as a preacher to the Borinage, the industrial zone where the miners existed under shockingly sad conditions. In this unspeakable destitution, van Gogh's inner compulsion to artistic expression originated, his way to art began here. His brother Theo, who later became a successful art dealer, took over his financial support, something which went on for the rest of his life since van Gogh never found a possibility to sell his paintings. He went through several stages in Holland, e. g. in the studio of his relative Mauve who taught him the technique of aquarelle painting. He also spent several months at the Antwerp academy where the regulations were unbearable to him. Eventually he came to Paris where his best time began. He met Toulouse-Lautrec, associated with the Impressionists from whom he got to know Japanese woodcuts which fascinated him and which made him look for completely new aspects in his paintings.

But living in Paris, with all his debating artist friends,, the distraction and the distance from nature was an encumbrance for the son of a farming community. He fled from the city and withdrew to Arles in the South, a countryside red-hot with sunlight. There he created the best paintings in his life. Vincent worked as if in a fever and at the same time dreamed of a creative artists' community. He asked Gauguin to come to join him in the yellow house in order that they might work together. But both artists lacked inner stability, and two such individualists were unable to work together. It came to a quarrel which coincided with van Gogh's nervous breakdown since he had based his whole life on his work without any consideration of physical fitness or mental strain. Still his encounter with Gauguin had helped his art to mature considerably. Both artists suffered harm by the argument but their works improved.

Van Gogh's health finally made it necessary for him to be treated in a sanatorium; he did not dare to work alone in his studio anymore. But even in those sombre surroundings, he created moving, beautiful paintings. It seemed as if his distress did not affect him deeply, "I work like a madman," he wrote, "I have a furious rage to work more than ever. And I believe that contributes to my health." But life with the other patients became unbearable. After a short stay in Paris he went to Auvers where he was able to live in the medical care of Dr. Gachet, an art lover who also had active contact with Cézanne and Pissarro. Dr. Gachet advised the sick van Gogh to work in order to allow the benefit of the spiritual edification, although his physical condition got worse and worse. In the end the catastrophe could not be held back. Van Gogh's psychic derangement also manifested itself in his pictures: he painted enormous wide fields with dark gloomy skies, his last painting shows black ravens rising from a cornfield which has been rooted by a storm. He wrote to his brother, "The future is becoming dark, and I can't look forward happily — my life has been grabbed by the roots and my step is faltering." Van Gogh put an end to his life. His brother who came immediately wrote, "The anxiety of an impending relapse or the crisis itself induced him to commit suicide."

Ernst Ludwig Kirchner
1880 Aschaffenburg — 1938 Davos

The architecture student E. L. Kirchner had completed three terms of an intermediate art course when he saw an exhibition of the French neo-Impressionists in Munich. He was so impressed that, on his return, he persuaded his fellow students Schmidt-Rottluff, Heckel, and Bleyl to give up their architecture studies and, with no reserve, start anew as painters. The four young people began to work with reckless enthusiasm. In summer they moved to the country and painted landscapes, in winter they painted nudes in their studio. They wanted to create directly from an artistic instinct, but of course they were not uninfluenced by the form and the colour of the Fauves.

The young artists decided to form the "Künstlergemeinschaft Brücke" which like-minded artists should join. Kirchner formulated in their programme, "to draw all revolutionary and fermentative elements together — that is the significance of the name 'Brücke'". In 1906, Max Pechstein joined the group. The five artists painted, discussed, and lived together, and it is therefore not surprising that it is difficult to distinguish between their works in those years. From 1911, the 'Brücke', worked in Berlin, where the mundane world of the metropolis gave Kirchner new themes. Cocottes, dandies, and demi-mondaines formed a shrill accent in his paintings, street scenes and milling crowds of people. Soon the Brücke group collapsed in the turbulence of metropolitan life. Kirchner became lonely and sensitive. World War I closed in upon a nervous over-sensitive artist, who first of all reacted with dispairing pictures but then had a nervous breakdown. After several stays in German sanatoria he went to Switzerland to find a cure. He visited Berlin again in 1918, but he found it strange and depressing. He moved to the Staffelalp in the Swiss mountains and shortly afterwards to a house in the Wildboden in the Sertigtal. His style changed several times, in the end one senses a trace of French influence, and he also came near various themes from Picasso. The fateful political development did not endanger him directly, but the discrimination against his works in 1933 hurt him deeply, especially as it happened at the same time as he received international acclaim in non-German countries. He was fatally ill when his paintings were removed as "degenerate art" in 1937 and committed suicide several months later. His work is, along with that of Max Pechstein, the most important example of expressionism in Germany. He was especially attracted to aquarelle painting twice: In his early days when he painted large colourful pictures of nudes and people and in his later works in Switzerland where he was inspired by the simple forms of a powerful landscape.

The paintings on the following pages:

97
VINCENT VAN GOGH
Boats on the Beach of St. Maries, 1888
Aquarelle. 39 × 54 cm
Lost
(Reproduced from a phototype with the friendly
permission of Piperdrucke, Munich)

98/99
ERNST LUDWIG KIRCHNER
Pine Trees in the Mountains (Wildboden), approx. 1924
Aquarelle on pencil sketch. 36.5 × 46.6 cm
Staedelsches Kunstinstitut, Frankfurt

100
ERNST LUDWIG KIRCHNER
Woodcart in the Forest
Aquarelle
Kunsthaus Zurich, Graphische Sammlung

Max Pechstein
1881 Zwickau — 1955 Berlin

Max Pechstein was the only "expert" when he joined the artists' community Brücke in 1906. He was a master pupil in the academy and had starved himself to pay for his studies as he had done previously for his apprenticeship as a painter and decorator. This training had given him the necessary qualifications for admission to the academy. Already in spring 1907 he was given the possibility to show his work in the first Brücke exhibition. "There was a wild shouting", he wrote in his memoirs, "not only in the Dresden press, but also in the whole artistic world. We were a welcome object of laughter and mockery for the good Philistines who only moved in the beaten track. But that didn't disconcert us. We felt proud to be carriers of a mission which was related to the art of the Dutchman van Gogh and the Norwegian Edvard Munch. The only art critic who declared himself for us was Paul Fechter."

Pechstein was able to travel to Italy on the proceeds of a state prize, which he had won during his time at the academy. It was mainly the early Italian works of art which entranced him, Fra Angelico, the mosaics of Ravenna, works of the Etruscans. A trip to Paris followed. There he was also fascinated by the early works in the Cluny museum and in the cathedrals. "But the thing which charmed me most was, although I avoided the rendezvous of the artists and poets, the life in the city on the Seine, its throngs of people. Etchings: a scene at the hairdresser's, whores, a labourer with his wife by a lamp-post, a man drinking liquor in a restaurant, a madam with her hands in her lap, people in a box at the theatre, a café, a cocotte."

A commission from Berlin ended the pleasant days in Paris, but it enabled him to live a modest life in the metropolis. Motivated by the many-sided experiences in Paris, he was now urged by the brisk life in Berlin, with its intensive lifestyle, to wild artistic activities. Impressive, powerful paintings were created at this time. Three of them were accepted for the exhibition of the Secession. "On the opening day I had a shock when I noticed how strongly and unmistakably my style forced itself to be noticed, compared to Impressionism." Walther Rathenau bought a painting, this enabled Pechstein to spend the summer on Nidden on the Courland Lagoon. The wonderful coast with its hardy race of people was to captivate the artist for years. Many of his best paintings, aquarelles, and graphics were created thanks to this inspiring landscape. A series of summer vacations on the Baltic Sea followed, on the Moritzburger Lakes, on hidden islands, and moors, in short, in the unspoiled nature, alone or with various artist friends. It was a time of unlimited freedom, filled with artistic creativity.

But the years of communal work irrevocably came to an end. Berlin with its complex way of life and diverse tasks for young artists forced Pechstein into isolation. The members of the group also went their own ways in their styles and views. Artists who were unaccepted joined together to become the 'Neue Sezession', Pechstein was among them. In this way, they created a possibility to exhibit which did not leave much profit but at least brought them publicity. Pechstein's financial situation gradually got better, he increasingly found buyers for his paintings. In 1913, he was able to make an old dream come true: a trip to the South Sea region of Palau, then still under the German flag. He found, "truly the paradise which I had been looking for. Each day followed the previous one in peace and tranquility: there was nothing which destroyed my peace of mind. No matter whether I observed the Palauans carving, fishing, hunting, or resting, my crayons always recorded their convivial lifestyle. Life was as clear and simple as the nature which surrounded me. It presented itself in unbroken, pure colours and in splendid, simple forms." His carvings were inspired by wonderful teak, he painted, travelled with the dugout, and eventually built himself a house in order that he could stay on these blissful islands. Then he received a message from the district commissioner demanding his immediate return to civilization: War in Europe.

Pechstein had not reckoned with such a turn in events, he had hoped that he would not be involved in this abandoned corner of the world. Sad, because of the events in his distant native country, he withdrew to his dwelling and attempted to ignore the facts and continue as usual. But, "in October my dream is finished. The Japanese are coming to the archipelago to take over command. I am suddenly an enemy from an opposing military force. I am kept prisoner in my house and eventually get free again . . . but it is over with work and peace, creating and observing. In October I have to leave everything behind." He started an adventurous return journey to Europe, taking the indirect route across the American continent. The last, long stretch of his journey, crossing the Altantic, was achieved by obtaining false papers and working as a coal trimmer on board a ship. He eventually arrived in Germany in 1915, where he was treated distrustfully as a deserter and immediately incorporated into the armed forces. He had to serve three years in the army before he could experience the feeling of release at the end of the war.

As soon as he was able to think of travelling again, he went to Nidden, worried that perhaps everything might not be the same as before: "much had changed, but it was pleasant to be greeted by the old fisherman friends. The fatal war had not been able to leave an impression on the water of the haff on the Baltic, or on the varying abundance of light in this North-Easterly strip of land, or on nature with its never-changing rhythm and its harmony of colour, which changed with the seasons. But I was still confused. I asked myself: how had I grounded the canvas before? What was my palette of colour? I had to gather my craft laboriously from my memory."

There then followed financial difficulties, as Pechstein's work had disappeared during his South Sea trip and unfortunate arrangements with an art dealer had robbed him of everything during the period of inflation. He did not despair, but always found strength for new creations. But it was the brutal suppression by the Nazis and destruction of his collection of works which he had built up a second time which wore the artist down. Ostracized, he hid himself away in Pomerania, stayed for years in a small hut on the Koser Lake, and lived from fishing. He was not allowed to work in Germany, nor allowed to accept posts which were offered to him from foreign academies. In September 1945, he stood in Berlin again in front of the ruins of his studio. It was a consolation for him to think of paintings which had passed into the possession of American collectors 20 years before. At least he could be sure that some of his paintings had survived this terrible time. Fortunately it became apparent after 1945 that a lot more of his work had survived than had been expected. Over fifty of his paintings are now on display in public museums in Germany. Many of Pechstein's friends were also able to smuggle paintings in their possession through the Nazi era. Many of his pictures are today in public collections in Switzerland, the Netherlands, and in the U.S.A., as well as in private collections in Germany and the rest of the world.

Max Pechstein painted lightly and quickly, otherwise it would not have been possible to leave a work such as his, considering the many losses. His best landscapes were painted on the coast, filled and penetrated with passionate feelings for all phases of nature. His aquarelles are no less assertive. They are sensitive and full of atmosphere, more lyrical than powerful.

The paintings on the following pages:

105
MAX PECHSTEIN
Fisherman's Cottages in Nidden, approx. 1919/20
Aquarelle. 49 × 64.5 cm
Private collection

106/107
MAX PECHSTEIN
Landscape in the Foothills, 1923
Aquarelle
Kunsthaus Zurich, Graphische Sammlung

108
MAX PECHSTEIN
The Artist's Wife, 1920
Aquarelle. 59.2 × 48.6 cm
Karl-Ernst-Osthaus-Museum, Hagen

Lovis Corinth
1858 Tapiau — 1925 Zandvoort

The term Impressionism, applied to German painting, is a little like a supporting corset, which is useful for statics but a hindrance for movement. One has got used to describing Lovis Corinth, Max Slevogt, and Max Liebermann as the main representatives of German Impressionism. While this is certainly true, it is unfair to the complexity of the artists and expecially in Corinth's case only touches a few facets of his lively work. It would be just as correct to call him an expressionist, or a Fauve. Form and composition structure were comparatively irrelevant in his paintings. He completely lived colour and was fascinated by movement and light.

Lovis Corinth found understanding for his artistic disposition from his parents which helped him through his difficult school years. After four years of study in the Königsberg academy, his experienced tutor advised him to attend the Munich academy where he was able to obtain sound knowledge in the craft of painting. What genius might be missing in the training — the young artist brought it with him. The conclusion of his years of learning was a study trip to Antwerp and a longer stay in Paris where he attended courses at the Académie Julian. The paintings of the Impressionists occupied him a lot; many of their perceptions, the colour palette, and their treatment of light and air were introduced into his work.

Corinth went back to Königsberg for four years before establishing himself in Munich in 1891, where he moved in the circle of artists of the Secession and "Jugend", without actually becoming one of them. His persevering work found recognition, his themes were many-sided. Apart from portraits, nudes, genre paintings and still lifes, he also tended towards Christian motifs and scenes from mythology.

In 1902, he moved to Berlin where he experienced highest artistic triumphs for a decade. He was one of the great artistic figures in the pulsating society life of the metropolis, respected and honoured. From 1915 president of the Berlin Secession and shortly afterwards professor, he also achieved external confirmation of his importance. In 1911, he became seriously ill, and with his physical disablement the contemplative nature in his work and scarcity of form, which distinguishes his whole late work, increased. The consequence of the weakening of his physical strength was a confinement to just a few themes from which he wrested artistic perfection in recurring metamorphoses.

Karl Schmidt-Rottluff
1884 Rottluff near Chemnitz — 1976 Berlin

Whenever one mentions discussions, experiments, or new methods in the circle of the Brücke artists, Karl Schmidt-Rottluff is described as a participant who observed the activities of the others with interest, did not say much, and who was more involved with his pipe than with his crayons. Later, when he stood in his studio in front of his canvas, he realized much more consequently from his inner tranquility what the others sought to achieve with hot-tempered discussion and engagement. "If one can talk at all about anything like an art programme", he said in an answer to an enquiry from a magazine editor in 1914, "then it is in my opinion something ancient and always the same. It is just that art is always manifested in new forms, since there are always new personalities — I believe its essence can't change. Possibly I am wrong. But I know of myself that I do not have a programme, just the indescribable urge to touch what I see and feel and to find the purest expression for it. I know that these are things which I can only come close to with art, but not with thoughts or words."

Schmidt-Rottluff was, among the Brücke artists, the one who was least affected in his artistic development and in his continuity by the internal influences of his friends or the external contemporary trends. "Seeing nature in large forms: that is the path which Schmidt-Rottluff has logically followed. Many of his early pictures, especially the woodcuts, can be described as graphic translations of negro sculpture into painting. The motifs are composed with hard, angular brushstrokes into harsh, sometimes unwieldy, coarse pictures. Deep cobalt blue, sulphurous yellow, and emerald green stand together in the colour treatment; or burning red is put against cold green, luminous blue against dull brown. There is nothing pedantic and nothing playful in these landscapes which were mostly painted in the North. His aquarelles are of a simple refreshing beauty. Nature literally flows into the framework of form: river and sea, the livid dunes and the moor aflame with colour." (Nemitz)

In retrospect, his work and the course of his life are more or less left untouched; the many-sided life in Berlin in the first 30 years of the 20th century had virtually no influence. He was a dominant member of the Brücke, close to his friends in the style and type of work done in those years. However, when the Brücke fell apart and Kirchner, for example, suffered terribly from the separation and got into difficult times with his work, hardly any reaction is reported on the part of Schmidt-Rottluff and no turning point can be noticed in his work. The following years of war on the Eastern front hindered him in his work, but after the end of the war he settled quickly into his accustomed way of life in that he spent the summer, painting near the Baltic, and the winter in his Berlin studio.

Schmidt-Rottluff is one of the few expressionists who remained true to the course which they had adopted, without losing themselves in fumbling experiments. "Simple and strong, often resplendent like nature itself, the colours in his still life and landscape paintings harmonize in a spiritual arrangement. The beauty of them is: they are familiar to the observer and at the same time always remain distant to him like the real picture itself. In the middle of a turbulent and labyrinthine present they bear witness to an unbroken and elemental feeling for life; islands of peace and tranquility." (Nemitz)

Recognition of his work by the public confirmed for him that he had adopted the right course, and the interest of serious collectors and influential friends made sure that he had no financial difficulties. In this way, his nomination to the Prussian academy in 1931 was consistent with his artistic personality. But two years later, Karl Schmidt-Rottluff, too, was overtaken by the disastrous political developments. He had to endure his expulsion from the academy which ended his fruitful teaching position, removal of his works in 1938 from German museums, soon followed by a ban on painting, and finally the destruction of his studio with the few remaining pictures. He was, as were his friends, a victim of the cultural downfall.

After the end of the war, when he finally was able to paint again, he picked up where he had been forced to leave off in 1941 and continued with his work in spite of the oppressive impact of the past, the depressing destruction and scattering of a great part of his previous work. In 1947, he accepted a professorship in the Berlin School of Fine Art and committed himself with devotion to conveying his vast knowledge to a newly-wakened young generation. In 1967 he made the foundation of the Berlin Brücke museum possible by donating works from his early years which had still remained with him and newer works from the post-war years. In this way, suitable space could be offered to the great period in which modernism emerged, to the works of his friends and his own contribution to these decisive years.

The paintings on the following pages:

113
LOVIS CORINTH
Walchensee, 1923
Aquarelle. 36.2 x 51 cm
Graphische Sammlung Albertina, Vienna

114/115
KARL SCHMIDT-ROTTLUFF
Ponte Nomentano, 1930
Aquarelle. 56 x 76 cm
Von der Heydt-Museum, Wuppertal

116
KARL SCHMIDT-ROTTLUFF
Girl, 1929
Aquarelle
Staedelsches Kunstinstitut, Frankfurt

Erich Heckel
1883 Döbeln — 1970 Hemmenhofen

The aquarelle has played an important, almost unchanging role in Erich Heckel's artistic activities. In his multitude of works it could take first place, and compared to his other paintings and graphics it is in no way inferior as regards content and artistic statement. Heckel belongs to the painters of the 20th century who have given weight and importance to aquarelle painting through the priorities which were established in this technique.

The artist obviously recognized early that painting out of doors did not suit his disposition. He only sketched outside, meagre metaphors of the essential aspects were memory enough for his visual understanding. He painted in his studio, especially aquarelles. Most important for him was the inner view of the respective motif which had formed in the artist's mind, the idea of form is his concern. At the same time, he never abandoned the reproduction of the visible world, something which was always fundamental to his painting. Aspects such as the representation of light and atmosphere — the major concern of the Impressionists — the inherent geometric substantiality of objects — chosen by the cubists as the main issue of their creation — and the detachment from physical reality — suggested by Marc and Macke, executed consequently by Kandinsky, these aspects were familiar to Heckel and were introduced into his painting, but subordinate to the picture of life. His work is, in general, characterized by a continuity in change: A collection of work which was subject to constant alteration was created without a break, achieved in logical steps by converting previous discoveries into a conscious will.

Heckel's artistic beginning can be identified with the foundation of the "Künstlergemeinschaft Brücke" in Dresden. Heckel, Kirchner, Schmidt-Rottluff, and Fritz Bleyl (who soon left) joined together in 1905 to realize communal artistic ideas. A common aim to live a new art united the young people, but they did not actually know what this art should look like. As Heckel later put it: "We knew what we had to get away from — but where we would arrive was not quite so certain."

The first years of working together produced a similarity in the artists' works, especially in their lithographs and oil paintings which makes a distinction of style difficult. This was not true for their water-colours where Heckel showed his personal style right from the start. Kirchner appears to have been the artistic leader in the initial stages of the Brücke while Heckel determined and positively provided for the spiritual climate. He was unquestionably the active businessman in the community, he acted as manager, organized the exhibitions, inspired, and set things in motion. The art which was formed in those years seems to a great extent to have been derived from the dialogue of the friends Kirchner and Heckel. It seems as if the artists had encouraged each other prolifically. However, the time in Dresden was short: the artists worked in the provincial town for six and a half years till they were no longer able to resist the move to the metropolis of Berlin. In Berlin, in the bustle of the many influences, the artists had to look after themselves in regard to their progress. In 1913, the Brücke was dissolved and the friendship between Heckel and Kirchner fell victim to a growing animosity.

The years in the group were an important time for Erich Heckel's artistic personality which matured during that time. It would, however, be wrong to view him just under the aspect of those years. Fortunately, he was able to remain artistically active and develop into old age. He served in the Medical Corps in World War I, and the emotional shocks of those years long continued to have an effect on his work. A new immersion in landscapes was liberating for him. The steep coastline of the Baltic was a great discovery. He found refuge in Osterholz near Glücksburg where he could retire to in the summer months. This remote area also enabled him to survive the Nazi regime, at the same time being able to work. In the course of time, the paintings of the Northern coast showed a lively union with nature which he had obtained. "It is obvious, especially in the drawings and aquarelles, that nudes and landscapes are not separate from one another, the nudes are not just accessory figures nor are the landscapes only scenery or background, but both, bathed in the same light and atmosphere, belong naturally and intimately together. To present naked human figures in nature was a main theme of Heckel's for a long time, it occupied him time and time again, and the summer days on the Flensburger Förde were very productive in this respect." (Köhn)

Apart from the summer stays there were extensive travels — as long as this was possible — above all to the Alps, which he was expecially attached to. In the winter months, he worked in his studio in Berlin. After his works had been removed from all public collections, and had been squandered or destroyed in 1937, bombs demolished his complete stock of paintings in his Berlin studio in 1944. He found refuge in Hemmenhofen on Lake Constance. This refuge became a permanent place of retirement which constantly offered him peace and the opportunity to work and also gave him space to produce an abundant late work. Heckel once wrote about a major exhibition of his paintings, "The artist, who sees large parts of his work from various periods unified, does not want to give the impression that he regards his work as final in any direction. He welcomes this display, because the modelled experiences form a new entirety and because every artist loves destroying over and over again the link with the past, no matter how obvious it appears after so many years. In this way, he can constantly remain a part of the oncoming generation."

Heinrich Campendonk
1889 Krefeld — 1957 Amsterdam

It is customary in Germany to classify Heinrich Campendonk as a member of the 'Blaue Reiter' group because of the incredibly creative years which he spent in the circle around Franz Marc. In the Netherlands, however, he is regarded as a Dutch artist, since he worked at the academy in Amsterdam after he had been expelled by the National Socialists. His artistic origin also testifies to his being Dutch. His tutor at the Krefeld school of arts-and-crafts, who decisively influenced his work, was the Dutch mystic Jan Thorn-Prikker, whose dreamlike images full of symbolisms were carried on by Campendonk.

In 1910, Campendonk made contact with Franz Marc through Helmut Macke, brother of August Macke. Marc was very impressed by his work, and he persuaded Campendonk to move to Sindelshof in the Bavarian foothills which had become a sort of summer meeting place for artist friends since Marc had his studio there. The years in Southern Germany were very productive, he learned a lot from Kandinsky and the other friends, and was, at the same time, the one who was familiar with a lot of the works of van Gogh, Cézanne, and the other French artists. He had acquired this knowledge from his tutor in Krefeld, and it was now eagerly absorbed by the young group. One should not forget that the acquaintance with French painting was still very fragmentary in Germany in the first decade of the 20th century.

Campendonk was dismissed from the military service for health reasons and moved to Seeshaupt on Lake Starnberg in 1916. The group Blaue Reiter had been intensively involved with the glass painting technique of the Alpen folk art. Influences from this had drifted into Campendonk's work and had led to a completely new form of this glass painting in his work. He transferred the linear ornamentation, abundant with inventiveness of form, in intensive translucent colourfulness, expecially into his aquarelles which accompanied him through his whole creative life.

In 1926, he accepted an appointment to the Dusseldorf academy, where P. Klee and H. Nauen also worked. He turned to stained glass windows with great success. This was an area where he received many commissions in the ensuing years. In 1933, his successful work in the academy was put to an abrupt end by the Nazi regime. The director and many of the artists were dismissed, many had to leave the country. Campendonk was able to establish himself in Holland, but the brutal treatment of his work had deeply injured him. He only allowed his work to be shown in public on very few occasions and withdrew, apart from his teaching activities, completely from the artistic world.

The paintings on the following pages:

121
ERICH HECKEL
Cress, 1925
Aquarelle. 65.5 × 53.5 cm
Leopold Hoesch Museum, Düren

122/123
ERICH HECKEL
Landscape in Angeln, 1932
Aquarelle. 55.5 × 68 cm
Landesmuseum, Münster

124
HEINRICH CAMPENDONK
Adda, 1919
Gouache. 39 × 34 cm
Galerie Beyeler, Basel

Oskar Kokoschka
1886 Pöchlarn — 1980 Villeneuve

Oskar Kokoschka is one of the three outstanding personalities who went the special Austrian way towards the art-historical upheaval of modernism at the beginning of the 20th century. Together with Gustav Klimt, whose pupil he was, and Egon Schiele, who died young and to whom he was connected by many lines in development, he is the artist who made his way from the productive artistic life of Viennese art nouveau to European expressionism. At twenty-five, he was already assured a place in the elite of European artists. He was at the centre of cultural life as a designer, painter, and expressionistic playwright.

Kokoschka began his career by studying at the Viennese school of arts-and-crafts and soon became a co-worker in the "Wiener Werkstätte". His literary work "Die träumenden Knaben" which appeared in 1908 with its legendary connection between art nouveau (Viennese style) and expressionism soon made him famous. Herwarth Walden discovered him for the "Sturm", and his first great expressionistic paintings were still created before World War I. He was seriously injured in the war in 1916, and in 1917, he was caught in a severe physical and mental crisis which exhausted him so much that he had to bear several long stays in sanatoria. "A person who is fighting to cope spiritually with depressing world events and his own infirmity and attempts to console himself with his work. He writes, draws, and paints with the utmost concentration." (Wingler)

There followed rich years of creativity with many travels through the whole of Europe. Kokoschka had achieved world renown as one of the greatest artists in the 20th century. The first phase of aquarelle painting also falls between 1920 and 1930. His knowledgeable biographer H. M. Wingler writes, "His late style is heralded at the end of the twenties by a superior, more conscious, freer use of the resources of composition. The angle of vision under which things in nature are offered is now in the work of art often extended or shortened so that characteristic features appear intensified; it is always a very essential statement which Kokoschka makes. His palette becomes lighter, his technique, on the other hand, changes, at the most, gradually. The human form again receives a prominent place in his choice of subject."

The world economic crisis imposed considerable restrictions on Kokoschka, and his ostracism by the Third Reich turned the cheerful traveller into a suffering emigrant who worked in the humanitarian field with unprecedented commitment. The aquarelle which had always played an important role became a technique which he increasingly used from 1941, and he devoted his creative energies to it for the rest of his life.

Henri de Toulouse-Lautrec
1864 Albi — 1901 Malromé

For his contemporaries Henri de Toulouse-Lautrec was above all a very impressive graphic artist, who had an incredible success with his bold posters. His pictorial work, however, was in the shade, much to the regret of the artist who created his posters with a light hand, but put all the energy he had into his paintings. The public lacked the sensitivity to perceive in his paintings the reference to the untenable conditions of life, they overlooked the signs of the beginning of a new epoch in painting, social criticism as a new content of art. Because of this a lot of his paintings were only very slowly appreciated by his fellow-man or accepted by the art critics. But even when the general public had recognized his genius and the meaning of his work, one of his former tutors, Bonnat, was able to prevent the acceptance of his paintings in the Louvre collection because of conservative considerations.

In the ensuing years, artists viewed Lautrec's work completely differently. They were works of art for them — especially the innumerable sketches — a rich source from which expressionism, still in its beginnings, was able to learn freedom of movement and keen precision. Together with van Gogh and Gauguin he became a forerunner of the Fauves. His explosive development of a new picture composition taking into consideration all the graphical effects, the further development of the impressionistic colourfulness and the turn to sociocritical themes made his work unique. At the same time, Lautrec had made virtually no comments on the theories of art. His way to art went from the absorption of the momentary atmosphere directly to the optical impression and from there to the sensitive representation. The indirect way of observing and considering theoretical principals of picture construction was foreign to him. This lack of interest in the academical foundations of art logically led him to devote himself to many tasks which, according to prevailing opinion, did not absolutely belong to the works of a serious artist. One of his great successes was, for example, the decoration of a fairground stall for the diseuse La Goulue. The theatre was also one of his great loves, which was perhaps a little unfortunate. His stage decorations regrettably had no success, not because they were no good or did not impress the public, but simply because of the mediocritiy of the plays which failed dismally. It is therefore understandable that because of his involvement with this milieu, which was tolerated but deemed unworthy, he was embarrassing as an artist to the conservative critics.

The life of this enormously talented young nobleman, who came from one of the most distinguished French families, was fateful and unusual. He was sickly from an early age, his growth slowed down, and as a grave symptom it had to be realized that his legs were very delicate. His bones did not become hard enough and could only take very little weight. As an adult, Toulouse-Lautrec had the normally developed body of a well-built man, resting on weak legs which had remained as short as in the growing phase of a child. But his long illness also had a positive effect. He developed his drawing talent, and as he was spared the military career which a person of his standing would have followed, he was able to obtain his parents' permission to take up the profession of an artist.

His entry into the Studio Cormon in Paris did not bring him any artistic gain, but was very important for the personal development of the young man. The studio lay in the middle of the aspiring artists' quarter of Montmartre; the lifestyle and the lively company of his young colleagues soon became an elixir for the insecure Lautrec. He worked intensively and at the same time indulged in an extensive night life, without paying attention to the dangers which he exposed his fragile physical condition to by this hectic work and lifestyle. He was a constant guest in the cabarets which were springing up everywhere at that time. There he found his motifs and models. The atmosphere in these establishments interested him more and more and increasingly dominated his work. Customers and participants in this nightlife interested him equally. He became familiar with the new coarse surroundings and found artistic maturity in his work within a short time. Unlike his friends, adherents of Impressionism, who favoured nature and the open country, he sought the haze of the night, the small space, the concentrated effect of the human maelstrom in an ecstatic turbulence. His brushwork and the nervousness of his pencil strokes increasingly resembled the adroitness of his chosen models.

Toulouse-Lautrec enjoyed painting aquarelles and opaque water-colours in various mixtures as the technique of aquarelle painting with its special forms of expression appealed to his interest in quickly catching a moving scene. He also liked the colour effect of painting on paper with transparent and opaque water-colours. He dedicated himself, with the same enthusiasm, to the potentialities of colour lithography, and within a short time showed his brilliance in this field as well. Lautrec the painter, designer, and lithographer always understood how to master those techniques and how to use them in such a way that allowed him to express himself as he felt at that particular moment. His genius proved itself in every genre and lent his work the homogenous character which is so particular to it.

The paintings on the following pages:

129
OSKAR KOKOSCHKA
Larkspur and Roses, 1967
Aquarelle. 61.6 × 49.5 cm
Marlborough Fine Art Gallery, London

130/131
OSKAR KOKOSCHKA
Summer Bouquet, 1965
Aquarelle. 62 × 49 cm
Marlborough Fine Art Gallery, London

132
HENRI DE TOULOUSE-LAUTREC
Cocyte in 'The Fair Helen', 1900
Aquarelle. 62 × 45 cm
Musée Toulouse-Lautrec, Albi

Maurice de Vlaminck
1876 Paris — 1958 Reuil-la-Gadelière

"My passion urged me to daring audacity against the conventional in painting. I wanted to evoke a revolution in habits, in daily life, to show the unrestrained nature, to free it from all the old theories and from classicism whose power I loathed in the same way as the power of generals or colonels. I did not feel resentment or hate, but a sort of rage ruled me, I wanted to create a new world, the world as seen through my eyes, a world for me alone."

Maurice de Vlaminck was one of the founding members of the Fauves, the wild beasts. He was an original personality and was certainly one of the group who heard the name with pleasure and found it appropriate. He did not just paint with enthusiasm, he also played the violin excellently — and participated in bike races successfully. His artist friend André Derain, a partner on the way to fame and world renown, remembered that one always saw Vlaminck engaged in one of his three favourite pastimes: he was either out with his easel, painting, or playing his violin, or cycling around blocks of houses. Everything he did was done with verve for the whole of his life. In later years, his passionate dynamic way became occasionally awkward for his contemporaries: His paintings were now more sedate, more beautiful, and less disturbing, but instead he set pen to paper and wrote essays, treatise, criticisms, and shocked more people than he had done in his younger days with his paintbrush. He also put away his racing bicycle but to the alarm of many now drove racing cars!

Until 1907, he stood completely under the spell of van Gogh. The crucial experience for him was the famous van Gogh exhibition in the Galerie Bernheim in 1901. He left the exhibition deeply moved and stated, "Van Gogh means more than a father or a mother to me." In 1900, Vlaminck had met Andrè Derain in Chatou, a Paris suburb, who lived there and who had already completed a training as painter. Towards the end, Derain had also received inspiration from Matisse, who he had met a year before at the academy Carrière. Vlaminck eagerly trained in this new style of painting: "The chance meeting with Derain produced Fauvism. People believed it referred to a bet, and a storm of indignation broke out in the artistic world, a general laughter seized the public, when they saw the paintings from André Derain and me, hanging on the walls in the exhibition hall of the Cours-la-Reine. The large areas of pure colour aroused general astonishment. There were opponents, partisans, and in the second year the initiated. The artists concerned were brought together in a hall and a name, whimsically proposed by one of them, was given to the movement: Fauvism."

Raoul Dufy

1877 Le Havre — 1953 Forcalquier

Raoul Dufy was a painter connected with the Fauves as well as with the cubists. But the charming pictures which people enjoy all over the world are the paintings from his later period, when Dufy created his own world of pictures without belonging to any group. "Dufy sought the beauty in the world with an obviousness which occasionally bewilders us or even leaves us uncertain. The decorative feature of his painting for which he was sometimes reproached, is basically an obvious love for the world and a self-assured craftsmanship which Dufy had made his own to bring this beauty into painting. He never avoided this confidence, this contrived technique, in fact he looked for it. His eminent paintings full of charm and joy appear to me to be a mixture of naive delight in observation and highest artistic refinement, like a joyous arabesque in the best taste and sense." (Hans Platte)

Dufy first began his artistic training in Le Havre in 1892. After completing his military service, he received a scholarship which enabled him to study in the studio Bonnat in Paris. Until 1905, especially the works of van Gogh, Gauguin, Pissarro, and Monet influenced his style. He studied together with Rouault, Marquet, Matisse, and Othon Friesz. With them he turned increasingly towards an expressive painting based on the power of colour and became one of the founding members of the Fauves, the wild beasts. But already in 1908, influenced by Cézanne, the form of the represented object essentially appeared in his work, the arranged landscape. Increasingly, the underlying geometric forms emerged from this arrangement and cubism came into being. Dufy remained true to the landscape even in cubism and around 1914 his conception of painting was consequently completely altered. The geometric element receded into the background, there emerged a completely new form of painting alive with colour and strong design, that unmistakable style which Dufy had remained true to. It became a pictorial language only related to him.

For a long time, the artist designed patterns for materials for an exquisite silk weaver, an area where he was very successful. The silk manufacturer invited Dufy to the fashionable horse races so that he could study the effect of his materials in the crowd. The atmosphere of the race track fascinated the artist, and many paintings were created which have themes from horse racing. The beauty of the landscape, but also the stimulating aura of the theatre and concert, of music and social company, the human figure, animals, and, time and time again, flowers — these were the sources of his art.

Paul Cézanne
1839 Aix — 1906 Aix

Paul Cézanne, son of a self-made man who from modest circumstances had risen to become a millionaire banker, could have led a comfortable life as wealthy heir on his inherited country estate, if he had had the normal interests of his class. But his desultary temperament prevented him endorsing an existence which he believed to be uneventful. After a short term of studying law, he was able to bring his father around to accepting his choice profession as artist, although he was much less successful in convincing himself that it was his vocation. He was tormented by doubts about his own qualifications till old age. When the public and the critics passed malicious judgement on his works at the third exhibition of Impressionists, although he had displayed sixteen of his best paintings, he was offended and withdrew from the artistic scene for a long time.

Camille Pissarro, with his relaxed and contented lifestyle the exact opposite of Cézanne's unstable uneasiness, was a constant, understanding companion for a long time, first as a teacher, later as a friend. Cézanne could only reconcile himself with the Impressionists for a short time. What his friends aimed for as fulfillment was not enough for him. Soon he was looking beyond the liberated colour towards solutions for formal arrangement, for spiritual content, and clarity in composition. He made many attempts at captivating the moving world of illusion in his paintings. The human figure, the still life, and the landscape were his themes. He freed himself from the thick colour application of his impressionistic years, investigated with subdued colouring the magic of form which is inherent in everything. Light and transparency became increasingly important to him and consequently he turned his attention to the aquarelle, which met with his views. He avoided black and resisted the temptation to make contrasts with the use of chiarascuro effects. He fashioned everything from the colour, without contours. He achieved his work through methodical observation of nature, "Here on the banks of the river, the motifs are multiplied; the same subject seen from another angle offers an object of study of the utmost interest and such variety that I believe I could occupy myself for several months without moving from the spot, but by just turning either to the right or to the left."

Cézanne had an enormous influence on modern art. He only believed in his own genius in his last years through the tributes paid to him by younger artists.

The paintings on the following pages:

137
MAURICE DE VLAMINCK
Southern Landscape with Village, approx. 1919
Aquarelle with pencil, quill, and Indian ink.
36.4 × 48.2 cm
Staatsgalerie Stuttgart

138
RAOUL DUFY
Le bouquet d'arums, approx. 1939/40
Gouache. 66 × 50 cm
Galerie Beyeler, Basel

139
RAOUL DUFY
Nice, La fête du Lou Mai, approx. 1930
Gouache. 65 × 50 cm
Galerie Beyeler, Basel

140
PAUL CEZANNE
The Boy with the Red Waistcoat, approx. 1890/95
Aquarelle. 46 × 30 cm
Sammlung Marianne Feilchenfeldt, Zurich

137

Pablo Picasso
1881 Malaga — 1973 Mougins

It is impossible to integrate Pablo Picasso's work into the history of artists, his contribution to modern art was too varied and many-sided. He created styles, then left them behind with no regret, when he was faced with new problems. He took up ideas from other artists, altered them and mixed together things which one thought incompatible. He worked in all disciplines of pictorial art, touched upon almost every known technique, and created several new ones. He always resisted any sort of pigeon-holing or classification. He wrote, "The different methods which I have used in my art should not be interpreted as a development or stages towards an unknown ideal in painting. Everything which I ever made was for the present, in the hope that it always remains alive in the present. I have never bothered about examinations. When I found something which I wanted to express, I did it without thinking of the past or the future. I don't believe that I have used totally different elements in the various methods of my paintings. If the objects which I wanted to represent required a different form of expression, I never hesitated to use it. If I had something to say, then I said it in the way that I felt it had to be said. Different types of motifs inevitably demand different methods. This has nothing to do with development or advancement but is rather an accommodation of the idea which one wants to express and the means of expressing this idea."

Picasso was born in Spain and always remained a Spaniard at heart, even though he lived in France, first out of inclination and later because of the political situation. When he began to work in France, he was definitely under the spell of van Gogh, and in his 'Blue Period' (till approx. 1904) the influence of Toulouse-Lautrec is present. He was also the key figure for Picasso's views on mankind. Already in his 'Rose Period' (till approx. 1906), the peak of which was the large painting of the "Demoiselles d'Avignon", other artists were looking to the ingenious Spaniard. He was now the one who inspired others. His studio in the 'Bateau-Lavoir' (Max Jacob had christened the derelict wooden house washtub) became the meeting-place for all the artists who were striving for new aesthetics in art. Here one can find the roots of cubism, here came the awareness of a new way of seeing things which for Braque, Juan Gris, and Picasso dissolved every-day objects in the studio into basic geometrical forms. The genius who as a youth already mastered everything he needed for his craft was supremely capable of meeting every artistic challenge for the whole of his life.

Maurice Utrillo
1883 Paris — 1955 Paris

Utrillo's path to art was unusual. His mother, Suzanne Valadon, was the much sought after model of Degas and Renoir, Puvis de Chavannes and Toulouse-Lautrec. This association with creative artists awoke an irresistable urge in her to draw, something which she did very well. She was encouraged by Toulouse-Lautrec and Degas and so integrated into the artistic scene as an active member. Her son Maurice grew up in the midst of turbulent relationships, he was left completely to himself, and while still a youth had already developed a dependance on alcohol. His mother eventually persuaded him to paint to get him away from the bottles of red wine. Considering that he was forced to paint without personal conviction and received no instruction worth mentioning, he painted amazingly original pictures. He was a natural talent. There now began a time of constant ups and downs, of creative periods and confinement in sanatoria. He was an immature drunkard, helpless and unstable, dependent on alcohol, and began to paint against his will — and as if inspired by a strange power, he was spontaneously able to paint "expert" pictures. Then another confinement in an institution for alcoholics was unavoidable. It was tragic that Utrillo painted his best pictures when he was under the influence of alcohol, and therefore his creative periods were inevitably set by this or alternatively by the break-down of his physical resistance. His motifs were the empty streets of Montmartre, its squares, bridges, bars, alleys — they are almost always portrayed without people, because he was shy of the crowds who had often made him a target of their mockery. "Utrillo loved Montmartre in intimate emptiness, asleep in village seclusion, the Montmartre which usually ruled Paris. There he could roam the streets without being spoken to by anyone; I often surprised him in his contemplation of future paintings; then he disappeared into the emptiness, hands in his pockets which were filled with everything imaginable; cigarettes, bread, mussels, liquor bottles, oranges — everything; depending on chance and the season of the year." (Gustave Coquiot)

In order to bring some life into the monotony of the streets and to capture the neglected condition of the houses in his pictures, he concocted mixtures of plaster of Paris with sand and glue. An indescribable charm thus passed into his paintings, the humblest, dirtiest wall was given a fascinating charm by his paintbrush. In the so-called "white epoch" he produced his most outstanding masterpieces which today are jealously guarded in the most important museums, then sold dirt-cheap by their creator. His art was a strange combination of a refined impressionistic technique and naive painting. He never allowed himself to be confused by theory, everything he had was given to him generously by nature.

Edouard Manet
1832 Paris — 1883 Paris

He was one of the crucial artistic personalities of Impressionism, and yet he never abandoned pictures depicting people, still life, and other traditional themes in painting. Manet succeeded in building a bridge with the past in his work without falling into a spiritual or stylistic dependence on the old masters. His works found early acceptance in the 'Salon' and good response from the critics. The young artists from the circle of Impressionists, which was newly forming in those years, were much less successful in obtaining opportunities to exhibit. They found Manet's generous compositions inspiring, while he, on the other hand, appropriated several elements of the Pleinair painting style which his attention had been drawn to by colleagues. He was first numbered among the circle of Impressionists who at that time was treated hostilely by the public, when he exhibited his painting ''Le Déjeuner sur l'Herbe'' in 1863 in the 'Salon des Refusés', an exhibition forum for critical young artists. This caused a scandal.

This painting marked the beginning of success in the artist's life: In the following years he was attacked by critics and by the public, but still his paintings attracted considerable attention and many buyers. The famous art dealer Durand-Ruel bought many of his paintings for a considerable sum of money; soon he was regarded the leading figure of French modernism. But nevertheless many of his paintings which he submitted to the Salon were turned down, for example his ''Nana'', a painting which he was inspired to by Emile Zola. The author defended the artist after the refusal with verve. ''There are a great many artists,'' Zola wrote, ''who today are regarded as being famous and for whose paintings one digs deep into one's pocket; but I wouldn't exchange one of Manet's paintings for all of theirs. The day will come, when none of those artists will remain: But Manet's painting will last.''

Another author who strongly supported Manet was Charles Baudelaire, who Manet had been friends with since the start of the sixties.

In his early years, the aquarelle took the place of a sketch in Manet's preparatory work on a painting, a role similar to a pencil sketch. His late work reveals several important and fully elaborated paintings, as well as a series of perfect pastels. A serious illness forced the artist in his last creative years to work in a sitting position or lying down; he then preferred pastel, gouache and water-colour. With his physical disability the handling of those techniques was easier for him than oil painting.

The paintings on the following pages:

145
PABLO PICASSO
Etude pour le vert galant, 1943
Aquarelle with quill drawing. 31 × 36.5 cm
Galerie Beyeler, Basel

146
MAURICE UTRILLO
Moulin de la Galette, 1923
Gouache. 23 × 30 cm
Galerie Beyeler, Basel

147
MAURICE UTRILLO
Le Lapin agile, approx. 1931
Gouache. 50 × 65 cm
Galerie Beyeler, Basel

148
EDOUARD MANET
Bouquet with Laburnum and Iris
Aquarelle. 35.1 × 25.6 cm
Graphische Sammlung Albertina, Vienna

146

Marc Chagall
1887 Vitebsk — 1985 St. Paul de Vence

A wayfarer between worlds — creating dreamlike images from the spiritual and earthly life of his Russian-Chassidic forebears, with an alert sense for the beauty of our present world: a modern painter whose power of spirit enabled him to transfer the piety and wisdom of an ancient people into the art of the 20th century. He combined childhood memories of the simple life of Russian peasants with clear-sighted impressions from the spiritual worlds, dreamlike fairy-tale figures with a sensually perceived beauty of present life. The various participants in his paintings are shrouded in vivid colourful picture compositions with a harmonious friendly aura. "Chagall's work is unique and inimitable, full of the melancholy and innocent faith of the Slavic soul which also transfigures the passion of the Jewish people without bitterness, a work, new in its astonishing technique, ancient in its spiritual attitude." (Maurice Raynal)

The deep religiosity which imbued Chagall and which provides the fundamental harmony of his work can be traced back to the Jewish belief of the Chassidim in which he and his whole clan are rooted. Chassidim teaching stresses the importance of sentimental values in religion and considers revelations of nature to be almost as important as the code of law. It sees God in all manifestations of the world and preaches devout communion with God, not only in prayer, but also in joy and in the love of life. This insight is important, if one wishes to understand Chagall's creativeness. A second factor is the profound attachment to his native land and the peasant life of his village. The experiences of his childhood must have been so intense that they remained with him for all his life. One can always find a motif from his past in the innumerable details of his paintings, either details of his homeland or his childhood. "In my thoughts, my soul returns home time and time again."

Marc Chagall first began his art studies in Petersburg till a patron and collector of art enabled him to move to Paris. The years in Paris from 1910 till 1914 were decisive for his artistic development. He returned to Russia at the outbreak of war. But although he was recognized and honoured as a successful artist there, in 1923 he moved back to France which he had come to love. Here he received the decisive inspiration to illustrate the Bible, which was very important for his creativity and personality. It was as if a floodgate had been opened, and the world can be grateful for paintings of singular beauty, of infinite profundity which arose from Chagall's interpretation of this theme that from this moment on became like a luminous thread running through his entire work. "I see the events of life and works of art through the wisdom of the Bible. A truly great work is imbued with its spirit and harmony. I am not the only one who thinks this way, especially not today. As the spirit and the world of the Bible take up a large space in my inner self, I have attempted to express this."

The threatening events of World War II made Chagall's situation as a Russian Jew increasingly precarious. The German invasion of France and the following collapse of the country caught him unprepared. His friends had difficulty, persuading him to leave the country, which had become a second home to him, even though he was in acute danger. He arrived in New York on the day when Russia entered the war. The events of the war increasingly forced dramatic themes and emphases on the sensitive artist. Nightmarish, melancholic pictures emerged; conflagrations, crucifixions, paintings entitled 'War'. In 1944, Bella, his companion for over 30 difficult years, died. She left behind a deeply depressed artist who painted large sad scenes in dark colours, often followed by paintings which had an apocalyptic foreboding. At the same time, he sought strength by turning to his memories of Russia which were now mixed with memories of Paris. An extraordinarily intense art arose from the sadness and the memories. "It is a particular kind of sadness. Far from withdrawing into itself, it spreads itself on the wings of imagination and inspires Chagall to paint the strangest scenes of his entire work. It is a mourning running away from itself, going astray, and eluding itself." (Cassou)

He longingly waits for the chance to return to France. He travelled to Paris twice and was moved to see his beloved city again. When he finally did return in 1948, the French nation honoured him with a major exhibition in the newly opened Musée National d'Art Moderne. Vence, the embodiment of Southern landscape, became his home. Another illustrious name was added to the many painters from the past who had made this country on the sea their home — this time a name from the present.

Chagall married Valentine Brodsky, called 'Vava', in July 1952. Her gentle and cheerful charm, her prudence and her directness brought this roaming soul back to equilibrium. "Chagall has now reached the harbour. He had experienced various joys and sorrows and lived through extraordinary and frightful political disruptions. At the height of his fame and good fortune, perhaps he would feel moved to take stock of his life and express his profound gratitude. And he does — in the cycle of pictures from Paris ... Chagall enters this subject wholeheartedly. He transfers his passionate love for Vitebsk to Paris. The artist does this consciously, he knows that he has to be filled with such a love for a place. He has to worship a place so to speak; he needs a Holy City. From now on, this is

Paris, even though he is still attached to Vitebsk which lives on in his heart. Thus one finds a snow-covered Russian village in one of his Paris paintings." (Jean Cassou)

There are few artists who have remained so consistently true to themselves as Chagall. Fate had pushed him around between three completely different cultures, Russia, France, and America, but as he created so much from memory and from his inner self, he wove all outward impressions into his dreams and reproduced them as fables and parables. Although he had contact in Paris with representatives of every modern movement, especially Fauvists, cubists, and surrealists, he never became one of them. Chagall was always Chagall. He once said, "I definitely do not want to be forced into any system or any sort of classification at any time." Another time, "I am against terms such as imagination and symbolism. Our inner world is the reality. It is perhaps more real than the visible world."

The work of Marc Chagall is poetry of an inestimable vast dimension made visible. It does not only include large paintings which stretch over areas of painted walls, even decorate festive halls, his miniatures are also excellent, his countless ceramics, sculptures, and mosaics. His aquarelle and gouache paintings, techniques which he used all of his creative life, have just as much intensity as his other paintings. He used them then mostly for preliminary studies of larger works, but did not execute them any less carefully. In his early years Chagall also worked a lot with etchings, illustrations for notable books such as the works of Gogol or La Fontaine — and especially the Bible. The major works of his later period, apart from the spacious paintings, are to a great extent stained-glass windows. The luminous power of light shining through the glass is like an atmosphere which amalgamates with Chagall's own joy in colour. If glass painting had not existed since the early Middle Ages, Chagall would have invented it, since it is so much his métier. Here, too, as in all other techniques, the work of art retains the same characteristic style, Chagall remains with his inimitable language of imagery. He said himself, "Often more words, more silence, and more doubt are concealed in paintings than can be expressed with language. Spoken words often detract from the essential and lead one astray . . ."

The paintings on the following pages:

153
MARC CHAGALL
Still Life with Flowers, 1949
Gouache. 78.5 × 57.7 cm
Von der Heydt-Museum, Wuppertal

154/155
MARC CHAGALL
Motherhood, 1925
Gouache. 51 × 66 cm
Musée National d'Art Moderne, Paris

156
MARC CHAGALL
Sun and Mimosas, 1949
Gouache. 79 × 57 cm
Von der Heydt-Museum, Wuppertal

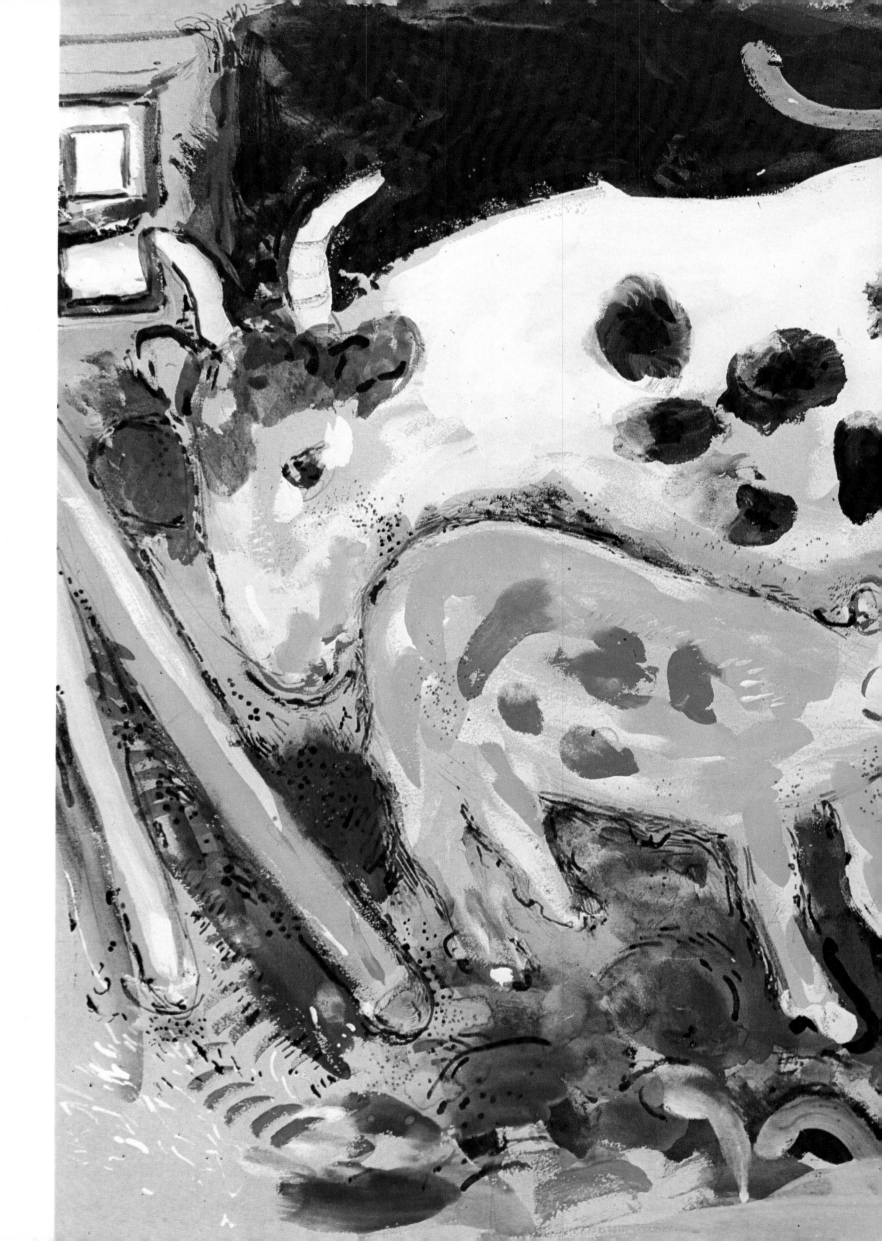

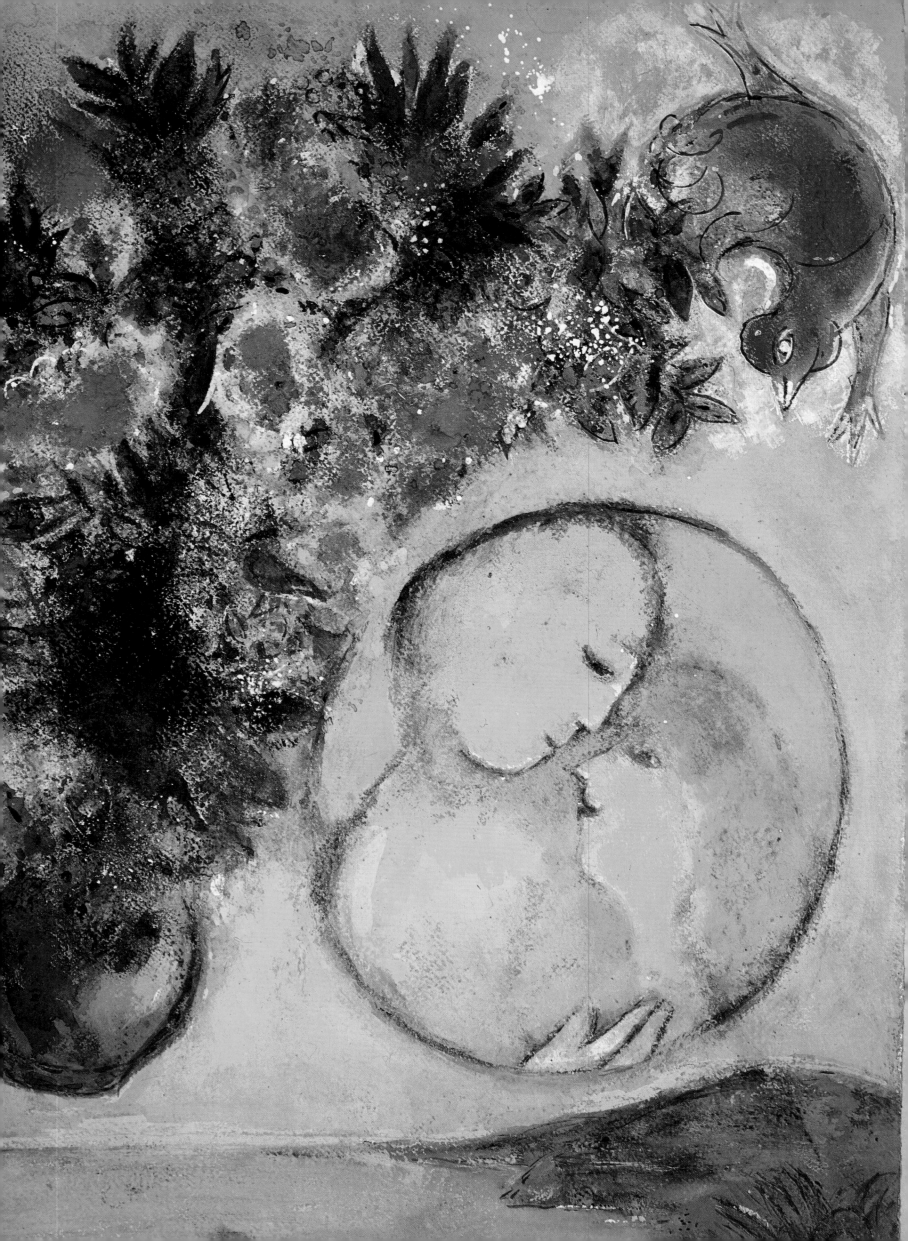

LIST OF ARTISTS

LIST OF ILLUSTRATIONS

Publishers and author thank the artists, the museums and collectors as well as holders of reproduction rights for the kind permission to publish the represented paintings.

Frau S. Mataré, Meerbusch: E. Mataré (p. 57)
Frau J. Schlemmer, Stuttgart: O. Schlemmer (p. 60)
Frau M. Feilchenfeldt, Zürich: M. Liebermann (p. 33)
Frau Prof. H. Rohlfs, Essen: Chr. Rohlfs (p. 89, 90/91, 92)
Herrn M. K. Pechstein, Hamburg: M. Pechstein (p. 105, 106/107, 108)
Herrn Th. Corinth, New York: L. Corinth (p. 113)

© Stiftung Seebüll Ada und Emil Nolde, Neukirchen: E. Nolde (p. 41, 42, 43, 44)
© Galerie Otto Stangl, Munich: F. Marc (p. 73, 74/75, 76)
© Dr. Wolfgang und Ingeborg Henze, Campione d'italia: E. L. Kirchner (p. 98/99, 100)
© Estute Erich Heckel, Hemmenhofen: E. Heckel (p. 121, 122/123)
© BEELDRECHT, Amsterdam / BILD-KUNST, Bonn: P. Mondriaan (p. 58/59)
© SPADEM, Paris / BILD-KUNST, Bonn: R. Dufy (p. 138, 139) P. Picasso (p. 145), M. Utrillo (p. 146, 147)
© COSMOPRESS, Geneva: L. Feininger (p. 49, 50/51, 52), M. Chagall (p. 153, 154/155, 156), P. Klee (p. 68), W. Kandinsky (p. 84), O. Kokoschka (p. 129, 130/131), H. Campendonk (p. 124), K. Schmidt-Rottluff (p. 114/115, 116)

Photographs: Photo Archives BERGHAUS VERLAG, Ramerding / Galerie Beyeler, Basel / Lichtbildwerkstätte Alpenland, Vienna / Fotoatelier Kleinhempel, Hamburg / Staatsgalerie, Stuttgart / Kunstmuseum, Bern / Archiv M. K. Pechstein, Hamburg / Verlag Schirmer-Mosel, Munich. The picture E. Mataré, Riverbanks was taken from the following book with the kind permission of the publishers: Erwald Mataré Aquarell 1930—1956 (Text by Anna Klapheck with a list of works by Ulrike Köcke, Munich 1983).